ECONOMIC DEVELOPMENT AND TRANSITION

In *Economic Development and Transition*, renowned development economist Justin Yifu Lin argues that economic performance in developing countries depends largely on government strategy. If the government plays a facilitating role, enabling firms to exploit the economy's comparative advantages, its economy will develop successfully. Governments in most developing countries attempt to promote industries that go against their comparative advantages, however, by creating various kinds of distortion to protect non-viable firms in priority industries. Failing to recognise the original intention of many distortions, most governments in transition economies attempt to eliminate those distortions without addressing firms' viability problem, causing economic performance to deteriorate in their transition process. Governments in successful transition economies adopt a pragmatic dual-track approach that encourages firms to enter sectors that were suppressed previously and gives necessary supports to firms in priority industries before their viability issue is addressed.

Justin Yifu Lin is Senior Vice President and Chief Economist of the World Bank. He obtained his PhD in economics from the University of Chicago in 1986 and returned to China in 1987, the first PhD in social sciences to return from abroad following the start of China's economic reform programme in 1979. He was the founding director of the China Center for Economic Research (CCER) at Peking University from 1994 to 2008 and is the author of sixteen books, including *The China Miracle* (1996) and *State-owned Enterprise Reform in China* (2001).

Economic Development and Transition

THOUGHT, STRATEGY, AND VIABILITY

Justin Yifu Lin

CAMBRIDGE
UNIVERSITY PRESS

CAMBRIDGE UNIVERSITY PRESS
Cambridge, New York, Melbourne, Madrid, Cape Town, Singapore, São Paulo, Delhi

Cambridge University Press
The Edinburgh Building, Cambridge CB2 8RU, UK

Published in the United States of America by Cambridge University Press, New York

www.cambridge.org
Information on this title: www.cambridge.org/9780521735513

© Justin Yifu Lin 2009

First published 2009

Printed in the United Kingdom at the University Press, Cambridge

A catalogue record for this publication is available from the British Library

ISBN 978-0-521-51452-1 hardback
ISBN 978-0-521-73551-3 paperback

Contents

Figures

Tables

Preface

Many improvements have been achieved in understanding the nature and causes of a nation's wealth in the past two and a quarter centuries since the publication of Adam Smith's *The Wealth of Nations* in 1776. It seems that many more improvements need to be implemented, however, before economists can truly be confident in providing advice to developing countries about their development and transition to a modern economy. The development policies adopted after the Second World War by a few east Asian economies were inappropriate in the context of the prevailing theories at that time. Those developing countries that followed prevailing development theories in formulating their policies failed to narrow the gap between themselves and the industrial countries. Similarly, China's transition to a market economy, begun thirty years ago, was thought doubtful in the light of prevailing theories. The path taken has led to sustained growth, however, while countries that followed standard approaches in their transitions encountered various difficulties.

This contrast in economic development and transition is intriguing to economists. I have had the privilege of experiencing in person the dramatic changes in China and carrying out in situ research of China's development and transition over the past twenty years. I have gradually come to realise that an economy's factor endowments, which are given at any time but can be changed through time, are an important starting point for the enquiry of economic development in a country. The factor endowments in an economy determine the economy's total budgets and relative factor prices – the two most important economic parameters at any given time. Moreover, given the preferences and available technologies in an economy, the structure of its factor endowments determines endogenously its optimal industrial structure. Any attempt to deviate from the optimal industrial structure will make favoured firms non-viable in an open, competitive market. Government subsidies/protection to these firms have to be maintained all the time, and their survival in a competitive world is not assured. Prior to the 1970s the prevailing social thinking ignored the endogeneity of industrial structure, and governments in developing countries were advised to adopt a strategy that promoted the development of advanced industry that went beyond the optimal structures, resulting in various institutional distortions and poor economic performance. New trends in social thought became dominant after the 1970s, however, as a result of the failure of previous models. The new social thinking advised developing countries to eliminate their distortions in a 'big-bang' manner so as to transit quickly to a well-functioning market economy. What the new social thought failed to recognise, however, was that the various distortions were endogenous to the need to protect subsidise non-viable firms in the old government strategy. Without addressing the issue of firms' viability first, the transition in many economies following the new social thinking was characterised by economic performance deteriorating from a 'second best' situation to an 'nth best' situation.

As the gap between the industrial structure of a developing country and that of an industrial economy reflects the gap in their endowment structures, it is necessary for a developing country to fill gaps in its endowment structure before it upgrades to a developed country's industrial structure by accelerating its accumulation of capital. Capital comes from the saving of economic surplus. If a developing country follows its comparative advantages, determined by its factor endowments, in choosing its industries, its economy will be as competitive as possible and it will be able to create the biggest possible economic surplus, have rapid capital accumulation and endowment structure upgrading and achieve economic convergence with developed economies. It is necessary for relative prices to reflect the relative scarcities of factors in the endowment structure so that firms operating in the economy choose industries and technology according to the economy's comparative advantages. Relative factor prices of this type can be obtained only in a well-functioning market system. Markets in most countries in their early stage of development are underdeveloped. It is therefore imperative for the government in a developing country to play an active role in building up market institutions in order to facilitate economic development. For a country that engages in the transition to a market economy from an economy with distortions arising from earlier mistakes in development strategy, it is desirable, as demonstrated by China, to adopt a pragmatic approach that liberalises the economy while giving the necessary support to non-viable firms before the issue of their viability is addressed.

The Marshall Lectures at the University of Cambridge on 31 October and 1 November 2007 provided me with the opportunity to summarise my research findings from the past twenty years. In addition to the text used when lecturing, I also included as an appendix a mathematic model to show that most distortions observed in the socialist countries and other developing countries are endogenous to their governments' strategy of accelerating the development of capital-intensive, advanced industries when their endowment structures are characterised by a relative scarcity of capital.

I would like to take the opportunity of the publication of these lectures to acknowledge the help that I have obtained from research collaborations with many friends and students over the past twenty years. Dr Cai Fang and Dr Zhou Li, my collaborators for various publications in the early 1990s, helped me understand the intricacy of China's economic system before the transition. My students Mingxing Liu, Pengfei Zhang, Peilin Liu, Zhiyun Li, Xifang Sun, Shudogn Hu, Yongjun Li, Feiyue Li, Zhaoyang Xu and Binkai Chen helped me at various stages to formalise my arguments and test empirically various propositions used in the lectures. The criticism and discussions of my observations with Professors Ho-Mou Wu, Demin Huo and Qiang Qong and other participants at the weekly development workshop at CCER deepened and improved my arguments. Many friends have also been kind enough to read earlier drafts of the lectures and to offer invaluable criticisms and suggestions. I gratefully acknowledge such help from Daron Acemoglu, George Akerlof, Pranab Bardhan, Gary Becker, Arne Bigsten, John Bonin, Pieter Bottelier, Hongbin Cai, Ha-Joon Chang, Kuo-Ping Chang, Ping Chen, Leonard Cheng, Partha Dasgupta, Alain de Janvry, Peter Drysdale, Manoranjan Dutta, Sebastian Edwards, Belton Fleisher, Robert Fogel, Bruno S. Frey, Richard Friberg, Benjamin M. Friedman, Ross Garnaut, Kai Guo, Sergei Guriev, Rong Hai, Yujiro Hayami, James Heckman, Bert Hofman, Haizhou Huang, Yasheng Huang, Athar Hussain, Grzegorz Kolodko, Deepak Lal, Frederic Langer, Keun Lee, Kyung Tae Lee, Wei Li, Deqiang Liu, Christer Ljungwall, Francis T. Lui, Albert Ma, Angus Maddison, Will Martin, Ronald I. McKinnon, Barry Naughton, Douglass North, Jeffery B. Nugent, Keijiro Otsuka, Elliott Parker, Dwight Perkins, Boris Pleskovic, Louis Putterman, Yi Qian, Mary-Françoise Renard, Chris Reynolds, John Riley, James Robinson, Gerard Roland, Christof Ruhl, Örjan Sjöberg, Ligang Song, Lina Song, Michael Spence, T. N. Srinivasan, Guofu Tan, Duncan Thomas, Yingyi Tsai, Guanghua Wan, Cheng Wang, Ning Wang, Yong Wang, Yi Wen, Xi Weng, John Whalley, Anita Yao, Shujie Yao, Shunli Yao, Shahid Yusuf and Hao Zhou. Maree Tait and Jan Borrie provided invaluable editorial improvements of the manuscript.

Justin Yifu Lin
Beijing, May 2008

ONE

Development, transition and divergence

The consequences for human welfare involved in questions like these are simply staggering: once one starts to think about them, it is hard to think about anything else.

Robert E. Lucas, Jr (1988)

When I was a student at the University of Chicago in the early 1980s I had the opportunity of observing Professor Robert Lucas prepare his 1985 Marshall Lectures. It is a great honour for me to follow Professor Lucas's steps to give the distinguished lectures twenty-two years later. I returned to China in 1987 after graduating from the University of Chicago and doing one year of postdoctoral research at Yale University's Growth Center. As the first person to return to China from abroad with a PhD degree in economics after the economic reform programme started in 1979, I have had the privilege of experiencing in person the miraculous changes in China's social and economic life and carrying out in situ research into China's development and transition over the past twenty years. Therefore, I would like to use this occasion to share with you my observations of developing countries' economic development and transition, based primarily on my experiences in China.

It is a well-known fact that, before the modern era, most countries were effectively in the development stage of a relatively backward agricultural economy – disturbed from time to time by war and natural calamities, and afflicted by the Malthusian trap. Except for the ruling classes, craftsmen and merchants – who represented a minority of the population – most people worked in agriculture. The allocation of resources in such agrarian economies was close to optimal through generations of practice; therefore, the gains from improvement in the allocation of resources were small (Schultz, 1964). Further economic development was feasible only with some exogenous technological shocks to the system. The accidental discovery of better technology during the daily work of peasants and craftsmen is one example of such a shock.[1] Another is the Great Geographic Discovery of America in the fifteenth century, which brought back gold and silver to Europe as well as new crops – such as maize and potatoes – with better adaptability to various soil and climatic conditions. In this pre-modern era economic development was manifested mainly in the form of population increase and the aggregate size of the economy. There was extensive growth, but per capita income did not change much (Clark, 2007; Kuznets, 1966; Perkins, 1969). The income gap between areas that today would be considered developed and those that would be considered developing was relatively small from today's viewpoint – estimated to be at most 50 per cent (Bairoch, 1993; Maddison, 2006). Some of today's developing countries – such as China and part of India – were believed to be richer than Europe at that time (Cipolla, 1980; Pomeranz, 2000; Smith, 1776 [1976]). Until the late eighteenth century the overall performance of markets – in terms of

---

[1] The adoption of certain technologies – for example, the replacement of the three-field cropping system with the more intensive two-field system in Europe – might be endogenous to the increase in population pressure, as argued by Boserup (1965). The invention of new technologies at that time came about mostly through accidental discoveries by peasants and artisans rather, however, than through purposeful research efforts (Needham, 1969).

integration – in China and western Europe was comparable (Shiue and Keller, 2007).

After the Industrial Revolution began in England in the mid-eighteenth century, experiments conducted in laboratories became the major source of technological invention and innovation (Landes, 1998; Lin, 1995; Needham, 1969; Rosenberg and Birdzell, 1986). This was especially true for those macro-inventions that consisted of radical new ideas and involved large, discrete, novel changes, as defined by Mokyr (1990). For developed countries at the technological frontier, such a transformation of the method of technological invention enabled them to accelerate technological advances through investment in research and development, and technological invention and innovation became endogenous (Lucas, 1988; Romer, 1986). With increasing investment in research and development, technology change accelerated, industrial structures upgraded continuously and productivity increased. As a result, developed countries began to take off and the divergence between the North and the South appeared (Bairoch, 1993; Baumol, 1994; Braudel, 1984; Clark, 2007; Clark and Feenstra, 2001; Jones, 1981; Kuznets, 1966; Maddison, 2006; Rostow, 1960).

Figure 1.1 shows the per capita income in various regions of the world from 1–2001 AD, based on the estimation of Maddison (2006: 642). It shows that, from an insignificant difference at the beginning of the eighteenth century, per capita income in the developed countries of western Europe and its offshoots had increased to more than twenty times that of the developing countries by the end of the twentieth century. As Lucas (1988) reflected in his 1985 Marshall Lectures, '[S]uch diversity across countries in measured per capita income levels is literally too great to be believed.'

It is natural for governments and people in poor countries to aspire to achieve the success of rich countries in Europe and North America. Except for a few newly industrialised economies (NIEs) in east Asia – as shown in figure 1.2 – most developing countries have

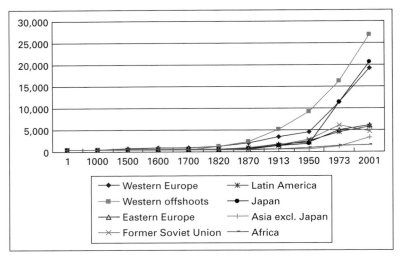

Figure 1.1 Per capita GDP of various regions, 1–2001 AD
Note: Gross domestic product (GDP) is calculated with 1990
international Geary–Khamis dollars. The Geary–Khamis dollar – also
known as the international dollar – is a sophisticated aggregation method
of calculating purchasing power parity (PPP), which facilitates the
comparison of countries with one another. The statistical definition can
be found at http://unstats.un.org/unsd/methods/icp/ipc7_htm.htm.
Source: Maddison (2006: 642).

failed to achieve their economic development goals since the
Second World War. In fact, many have encountered frequent crises,
despite the efforts of their governments and assistance from international development agencies such as the World Bank and the United
Nations Development Programme.

In most developing countries, after the Second World War, governments adopted various policy measures to promote industrialisation (Chenery, 1958, 1960, 1961; Krueger, 1992; Lal, 1983). At that
time most economists were expecting to see rapid growth in the
resource-rich countries of Africa and Latin America, but the real
success stories appeared in east Asia, where the endowment of
natural resources was extremely poor. Japan was the first success, followed by South Korea, Taiwan, Hong Kong and Singapore – the four

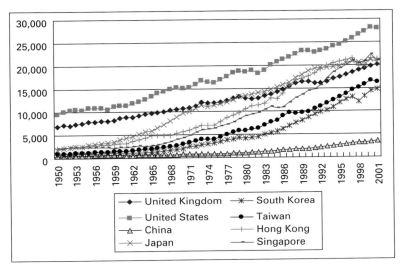

Figure 1.2 Per capita GDP of the United States, the United Kingdom
and the east Asian NIEs, 1950–2001
Note: GDP is calculated with 1990 international Geary–Khamis dollars.
Source: Maddison (2006).

east Asian NIEs – and, recently, by Malaysia, Thailand and
Indonesia. In these economies, in the early 1950s, their per capita
GDP of less than 2,000 international Geary–Khamis dollars – as
measured by the 1990 purchasing power parity – was the same as
China and less than that in eastern Europe and Latin America at that
time. The economies of the four east Asian NIEs maintained an
annual growth rate of some 10 per cent for two to three decades from
the 1960s. Such growth completely changed the poor and backward
state of their economies. Figure 1.2 shows that – as measured by
PPP – income levels in Japan in the 1970s and in Singapore and
Hong Kong in the 1990s surpassed that of the United Kingdom.
More importantly, wealth distribution in these economies became
more equitable during their economic growth (Fei, Ranis and Kuo,
1979). To some extent, these east Asian economies have realised
their long-pursued goal of catching up developed countries and
building equitable societies – a dream championed by many

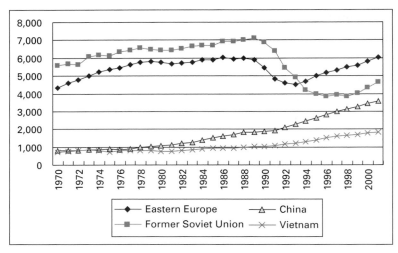

Figure 1.3 Per capita GDP of China, Vietnam, eastern European countries and the former Soviet Union, 1970–2001
Note: GDP is calculated with 1990 international Geary–Khamis dollars.
Source: Maddison (2006).

revolutionary leaders and social elites in developing countries, such as Vladimir Lenin, Sun Yat-sen, Mao Zedong, Jawaharlal Nehru and Gamal Abdel Nasser.

Since the late 1970s China and other socialist countries that had previously implemented a planned economic system began the transition to a market economy in order to improve their economic performance. Figure 1.3 shows that such a transition brought about rapid economic growth in China and Vietnam for more than two decades. The transitions that began in the early 1990s in the former Soviet Union and eastern European countries, however, led to dramatic declines in their economies and deterioration in most aspects of social development (World Bank, 2002a). A survey conducted in 2006 by the European Bank for Reconstruction and Development (EBRD, 2007) and the World Bank of 29,000 people in twenty-nine countries – including eastern and south-eastern Europe, the Baltic states, the Commonwealth of Independent States and Mongolia – found that only 30 per cent believed their lives were better than in

1989. During the same period most developing countries in other parts of the world followed the advice of the International Monetary Fund (IMF) and the World Bank to implement reforms to reduce government intervention and enhance the role of the market. The result was disappointing, however. The economic performance of most developing countries deteriorated during this period (Barro, 1998; Easterly, 2001a).

Continuous technological innovation and upgrading of industrial structures – as well as corresponding institutional changes – are the driving forces of long-term economic growth in modern times (Hayami and Godo, 2005; Kuznets, 1966; Landes, 1969; Marx, 1867–94 [1977–81]; Rosenberg and Birdzell, 1986). By borrowing technology and institutions, a developing country has the advantage of backwardness (Gerschenkron, 1962; Landes, 1969; Veblen, 1915). Like Germany, France and other countries in western Europe in the nineteenth century and Japan and the NIEs in east Asia after the Second World War, a developing country can learn from the experiences of developed countries in technology and institutions. Similarly, transitional countries, such as China and Vietnam, can also emulate the well-functioning market institutions of developed countries. This advantage enables them to undertake rapid technological improvements, upgrade their industry and adapt institutions at a relatively low cost and with less risk. Such an advantage can enable developing and transitional countries to maintain rapid economic growth for several decades, narrow the gap with developed countries and even overtake some of them.

While western European countries in the late nineteenth century and Japan and the NIEs in east Asia after the Second World War developed successfully and China and Vietnam succeeded in achieving rapid growth during their transition periods, why have most other developing and transitional countries failed to exploit such potential fully? This is the question that I explore in the following chapters.

TWO

The search for a fundamental and changeable cause of prosperity

But, soon or late, it is ideas, not vested interests, which are dangerous for good or evil.

John Maynard Keynes (1935)

The dominant social thought shapes the institutionalized order of society . . . and the malfunctioning of established institutions in turn alters social thought.

Theodore W. Schultz (1977)

How to develop a country is a subject that Adam Smith analysed in *The Wealth of Nations*, the publication of which in 1776 marked the birth of modern economics. The very diverse performances in economic development among various developing countries and in the transition of various socialist countries have recently revived economists' interest in economic development.

Recent studies have tried many ways to identify the determinants of economic growth in a country and have proposed various theories to explain why a country becomes wealthy and what actions a government in a poor country can take to improve its economic performance. Looking at the issue from an accounting perspective, the differences in per capita income between countries can be explained

by the differences in their physical capital, human capital and productivity. From this point of view, the way for a country to become
rich is to invest in physical and human capital and to adopt new and
better technologies. Such differences are just the proximate causes of
the income differences between countries, however, as the accumulation of physical and human capital and productivity growth are
themselves endogenous (Acemoglu, Johnson and Robinson, 2005;
Lewis, 1955; Rodrik, 2003). It is necessary, therefore, to look for
other fundamental factors that underpin the proximate causes of
income differences between countries.

Economists have proposed many fundamental determinants for
the economic performance of a country. Acemoglu (2007a) classifies
these into four main causes. The first is luck: uncertainty, hetero-
geneity in coordination, credit markets and government policies can
enable one country experiencing otherwise identical conditions to
another to escape poor equilibrium (Blanchard and Summers, 1987;
Howitt and McAfee, 1988; Krugman, 1981, 1987, 1991; Leibenstein,
1957; Matsuyama, 1991; Murphy, Shleifer and Vishny, 1989; Myrdal,
1968; Nelson, 1956; Rosenstein-Rodan, 1943). The second is geography, which affects the proximate causes of growth through soil
fertility, the availability of certain key resources, the disease environment, transportation costs and so on (Diamond, 1997; Myrdal,
1968; Pomeranz, 2000; Sachs and Warner, 1997, 2001). The third
factor is institutions, which shape the incentives to work and to
invest in technology and physical and human capital (Acemoglu,
Johnson and Robinson, 2001, 2002, 2005; Dollar and Kraay, 2003;
Easterly, 2001b; Easterly and Levine, 2003; Needham, 1969; North,
1981, 1990; North and Thomas, 1973; Olson, 1982; Rodrik, 2003;
Roland, 2007; Rosenberg and Birdzell, 1986). The fourth factor is
culture and social capital, including beliefs, values, preferences
and trust, which affect people's attitudes towards wealth, occupa-
tions, creativity and cooperation with others (Abramovitz, 1995;
Bockstette, Chanda and Putterman, 2002; Chanda and Putterman,

2007; Greif, 1994, 2004; Lal, 1998, 2005; Landes, 1998; Mokyr, 1990; North, 1994; Putnam, 1993; Weber, 1930).

Rodrik (2003) classifies the fundamental determinants of the economic performance of a country into three categories. In addition to geography and institutions in Acemoglu's list, he adds integration or trade, which is supported by empirical evidence from studies by Dollar (1992), Edwards (1998), Frankel and Romer (1999) and Sachs and Warner (1995) and which is advocated strongly by international organisations, including the World Bank, the IMF, the World Trade Organization (WTO) and the Organisation for Economic Co-operation and Development (OECD).

Luck as a fundamental determinant of income divergence in the long run is theoretically sound in models with multiple equilibria. The more relevant question, however, is why the government and people of a country trapped in poor equilibrium would not change their behaviour or improve their coordination to shift from a bad equilibrium to a good equilibrium. In fact, we have seen that some countries that have been trapped in poverty for centuries suddenly embark on dynamic growth, such as the east Asian NIEs in the 1960s and China after the reforms begun in 1979. What, then, is the factor that triggers the sudden change?

Although geography is the only exogenous variable in the list of fundamental determinants, it is not destiny (Rodrik, 2003). Most of Australia is arid, desert or tropical land; Singapore and Mauritius are tropical countries; Switzerland and Botswana are landlocked. All these conditions are considered disadvantages for long-term economic growth in the geography hypothesis; Switzerland, Australia and Singapore are among the world's richest countries, however, and Mauritius and Botswana have enjoyed dynamic growth in recent decades. European countries in the eighteenth century and earlier were plagued with many diseases (Clark, 2007): it was economic development that enabled them to eradicate these diseases and improve their environment. The impoverished environment in poor countries is, therefore, a consequence and not a cause of their failure to achieve economic development.

Some economists regard trade and integration – or, more precisely, government policy towards trade – as a fundamental determinant. It is true that successful countries have benefited from trade and foreign direct investment. Careful examination of the empirical evidence, however, shows that specific public policies directed at international economic integration or disintegration do not correlate well with economic performance (Rodríguez and Rodrik, 2001). Moreover, I will argue in these lectures that trade or the openness of a country is endogenous to the government's development strategy. Trade should not, therefore, be considered as a fundamental determinant of long-term growth in a country.

The proponents of the culture hypothesis argue that, through its effects on shaping people's attitudes towards work, leisure, risk, education, creativity and trust in other people, a country's culture determines its economic performance. Culture is a given or slowly changing factor, however. The difficulty with taking culture as the fundamental determinant of economic development is that it cannot explain why a country suddenly starts to take off after a period of long stagnation – such as the NIEs in east Asia in the 1960s and China and India after the 1980s. Neither can it explain why countries with the same culture – such as South Korea and North Korea, as well as West and East Germany – have dramatic differences in economic performance. Moreover, culture can change as a result of economic development – rather than being a cause of it. The hard-working attitude of Japanese workers has been impressive and is praised throughout the world today, but a quotation from a report written in 1915 by an Australian expert invited by the Japanese government to visit the country will suffice to illustrate the above point:

> My impression as to your cheap labour was soon disillusioned when I saw your people at work. No doubt they are lowly paid, but the return is equally so; to see your men at work made me feel that you are a very

satisfied easy-going race who reckon time is no object. When I spoke to some managers they informed me that *it was impossible to change the habits of national heritage*. (cited in Bhagwati, 1984; emphasis added)

Economists working on development and transition have come to believe that institutions – which shape the incentives of a society – are the fundamental determinant of economic performance and long-run growth in a country. They believe that a country will have dynamic growth and become rich if it has good institutions that provide incentives for work, accumulate human and physical capital, acquire better technology and improve resource allocation. If a country has poor institutions, which deprive people of the incentives to do the right thing for economic growth, it will be poor and will stagnate. Institutions are endogenous, however, and are determined by other social, economic and political factors in the economy (Binswanger and Ruttan, 1978; Friedman, 2005; Hayami and Ruttan, 1985; Lin, 1989; Lin and Nugent, 1995; Marx and Engels, 1848 [1969]; North, 1981; North and Thomas, 1973). Moreover, most institutions constitute a slowly changing factor although a few institutions may be able to change quickly (Roland, 2007). For the proponents of the institutional hypothesis, therefore, two questions need to be answered. First, what causes some countries to have good institutions and others to have bad institutions? Second, without significant changes to their bad institutions, why do some countries start to achieve a new path of dynamic growth?

The proponents of the institutional hypothesis focus their studies mostly on the first question and approach the issue from the conflicts of vested interests. Olson (1982) emphasises the effect on institutions from the growth of distributional coalitions in a country, which is a function of the duration of stability in a country. He argues that as time goes on without a revolution or other upheaval in the social structure, more and more special interests will form successful coalitions for rent seeking, and a society will become increasingly 'sclerotic' because of this and because of the growth of bureaucratic sluggishness within the special-interest organisations themselves.

Shleifer and Vishny (1993, 1998) and Grossman and Helpman (1996, 2001) see the structure of government regulations and interventions in a country as a result of political equilibrium, in which special-interest groups bid for protection with their campaign support and politicians maximise their own welfare. Such equilibrium depends on the total contributions collected and the welfare of voters. Using trade policy as an illustration, they argue that the special-interest groups may prefer inefficient distortions over more efficient means to transfer income.

Based on the studies of economic development in the New World of North and South America, Acemoglu, Johnson and Robinson (2001, 2002, 2005) propose that, in places where European settlers faced high mortality rates, they could not settle and were more likely to set up extractive institutions, whereas in places with low mortality rates they formed neo-European societies with institutions carried from Europe. These institutions, bad and good, persist to the present.

Similarly, based on the early history of colonies in the New World after the sixteenth century, Engerman and Sokoloff (1997) emphasise the pervasive influence of factor endowments on the quality of institutions. According to their argument, colonies that were endowed with climates and soils that gave them a comparative advantage in the plantation of sugar and coffee – lucrative crops at that time – or were rich in minerals for extraction used a large number of slave labourers because of the economies of scale in using such labour. The powerful colonial elites were able to establish social and political institutions that guaranteed them disproportional shares of political power and income distribution, in order to maintain their status, at the cost of economic growth – which Engerman and Sokoloff (1997, 2005) argue is the case in Latin America. Meanwhile, they argue that the soil and climate in what became the United States and

Canada were not favourable for large-scale plantation and mineral production. Further, since there was no large native population to provide labour, the development of the United States and Canada depended mostly on labourers of European descent, who had relatively high and similar levels of human capital. Due to the limited advantages of large-scale production of grain and hay, the distribution of land was more even. Consequently, the distribution of wealth and political power was more equal. These contributed to the formation of institutions that provided the population with broader access to economic opportunities, and incentives for investment in human and physical capital and technology, enabling the United States and Canada to sustain long-run growth and prosperity.[1]

While the importance of institutions is undeniable and vested-interest groups may influence the formation of institutions – as proposed by Olson (1982), Shleifer and Vishny (1993, 1998), Grossman and Helpman (1996, 2001), Acemoglu, Johnson and Robinson (2001, 2002, 2005) and Engerman and Sokoloff (1997, 2005) – the question of why the growth in some countries suddenly takes off remains unanswered. As already discussed, countries such as the east Asian NIEs after the 1960s, Chile after the 1970s and China, Vietnam and India after the 1980s, which escaped the poverty trap and started a new era of dynamic growth, did not have observable changes in the duration of their social stability or the deprivation of the elite's political and economic powers – at least in the beginning. Moreover, socialist countries with initially similar powerful vested-interest groups have adopted different transitional institutions and have achieved dramatically different economic performances in

---

[1] The vested-interest group hypothesis proposed by Acemoglu, Johnson and Robinson (2001, 2002, 2005) and Engerman and Sokoloff (1997) may not be valid for explaining Latin America's poor economic performance, as economic performance in Latin America lagged behind that in North America only after Latin America had adopted an import substitution strategy in the 1930s, and also because many institutional distortions arising from the import substitution strategy, such as the depression of agricultural and mineral prices, were harmful to the interests of the ruling landed elites there.

their transitions to a market economy. We need, therefore, to search for other fundamental but changeable determinants.

I agree with Keynes (1935 [1964]: 384) when he writes as the last, concluding sentence in *The General Theory of Employment, Interest, and Money*: 'But, soon or late, it is ideas, not vested interests, which are dangerous for good or evil.' The hypothesis I would like to propose is as follows.

The various institutions that hinder economic development in most former socialist and developing countries today are shaped by their governments, which followed inadequate ideas in line with the dominant social thought of their times about the priority development of capital-intensive, heavy industry in the 1950s when capital in their economies was scarce. The failure of many former socialist and developing countries to achieve dynamic growth in their transitional processes is due also to their governments' specific transition strategy based, again, on inadequate ideas in the form of the prevailing social thinking of those times, which ignored the existence of a large number of non-viable firms in the economy, and the fact that the distorted institutions that existed before the transition were, in fact, second-best arrangements for protecting these non-viable firms.

The government is the most important institution in any country, as membership in a state is universal, and the state has powers of compulsion over its citizens not given to other economic organisations (Stiglitz, 1989). Because of its compulsive power, the government has a substantial degree of freedom in adopting policies that will affect the functions of other institutions in society. With good use of its power, a developing country government can gradually reform its backward, growth-hindering institutions so as to improve incentives for entrepreneurs and workers, to increase savings and accumulation in the national economy for investment in new industries and technologies, and to improve resource allocation efficiency in the economy. It can also encourage and facilitate enterprises to learn from developed countries and to upgrade the country's industrial structures and technology. On the other hand, with incorrect use of its power, the government in a developing country can create distortions in the system and consequently hurt incentives for entrepreneurs and workers. It can further distort resource allocation and create rampant rent-seeking behaviour, causing unequal income distribution and giving rise to low efficiency and frequent economic and financial crises. The policies adopted by a government are, therefore, key to the success or failure of that country's economic development. As Lewis (1955: 376) insightfully observes, '[N]o country has made economic progress without positive stimulus from intelligent governments . . . on the other hand, there are so many examples of the mischief done to economic life by governments that it is easy to fill one's pages with warnings against government participation in economic life.' This is especially true in developing countries, as the constraints on government power are generally weaker than in developed countries. A more interesting question, therefore, is whether the government has the incentive and ability to design and introduce suitable institutions to facilitate the economic development of the country.

Political leaders operate the government. If we want to analyse the quality of a government's policies and regulations, we need to understand what motivates the political leaders in determining government policies (Lin, 1989).[2] A political leader certainly worries about, firstly, the security of his/her tenure[3] and, secondly, his/her own

---

[2] Lewis (1955) also emphasises the role of political leaders in a country's development. The case study of Botswana by Acemoglu, Johnson and Robinson (2003) finds that a number of far-sighted decisions by post-independence political leaders shaped good institutions, which in turn has helped Botswana achieve an average annual growth rate of more than 9 per cent since independence in 1965. Empirically, it has been found that an exogenous change in the national leader has a significant impact on a country's growth rate, from a panel data set including 130 countries since the Second World War (Jones and Olken, 2005).

[3] I define the term 'tenure' in a broad sense. In some developing countries, a political leader can exert his/her authority even after he/she retires from a formal office. For example, Deng Xiaoping did not have any official title after 1989; he was the de facto top leader in China up to his death in 1997, however.

position in the nation's history. Regardless of the political system, the best way to achieve security of tenure and to establish a leader's historical status is to bring prosperity to the nation.[4] As Alfred Marshall (1920: xvii) puts it, '[E]conomic motives are not exclusively selfish. The desire for money does not exclude other influence; and may itself arise from noble motives.' The motivations and behaviour of political leaders are not necessarily shaped by narrow, selfish, pecuniary interests.[5]

I argue in the next chapter that many political leaders in developing countries in the 1950s and 1960s – especially the first-generation leaders who brought political and economic independence to their countries through long periods of revolution or struggle – were motivated by their intrinsic desire for their nation's modernisation rather than by their own selfish vested interests.[6] In pursuing modernisation, political leaders in developing countries adopted certain strategies[7] – which consisted of a set of policies, including various interventions and regulations – as a vehicle to achieve their goals. The set of policies shaped the development and quality of institutions in their countries, which in turn affected their economic performance.[8] The strategy adopted by political leaders

---

[4] If a political leader's security of tenure is under threat, however, the leader may treat that security of tenure as a priority and adopt measures to safeguard his/her tenure at the costs of the nation's prosperity and his/her own status in history. Therefore, there is no guarantee that a political leader will indeed adopt policies to promote the nation's prosperity.

[5] If a political leader has security of tenure and high status in history, he/she will have almost everything – fame, respect and good living. Therefore, compared to the concerns of tenure security and high status in history, the concern of pecuniary gain should be almost nothing for most political leaders. If a political leader is unable to achieve tenure security and high status in history, however, he/she may become acquisitive and develop a 'grabbing hand' (see appendix 1) during his/her term in office so as to accumulate enough wealth for his/her living and other needs after stepping down from office.

[6] A good example is that, in the socialist revolutions in China and many other countries, most revolutionary leaders came from bourgeois families.

[7] My definition of 'strategy' is similar to that of Rodrik (2005).

[8] The bureaucrats in lower levels of government in a developing country may subsequently use the interventions/regulations that are endogenous in the development

was influenced by the dominant social thought at the time, which – as defined by Schultz (1977) – consisted of various social, political and economic ideas about the roots of the problems with existing systems and alternatives for the future. Due to the complex nature of modernisation in a developing country and the political leaders' bounded rationality in understanding the subject, it was practical for political leaders to follow the dominant social thought in the pursuit of national development. Moreover, following the prevailing social thought made it easier for political leaders to mobilise public support for their policies. As argued by Schultz, therefore, it was the dominant social thinking that shaped the institutional order of developing countries.[9]

My argument, however, is that the dominant social thought about achieving modernisation in the 1950s and 1960s was based on incorrect perceptions of the root causes for and constraints on a developing country's modernisation. Except for a few economies in east Asia, which escaped the influences of the dominant social thinking at that time, the established institutions in developing countries performed poorly. They not only failed to deliver the promise of making their countries as successful as developed countries, but also caused stagnations, frequent crises and even disastrous consequences in their economies. The failure of pursued economic strategies and their related institutions in turn altered the prevailing social thought and led developing countries – socialist and non-socialist alike – to start the institutional reforms and transitions that occurred in the 1980s,

Footnote no. 8 (*cont.*)

 strategy for their personal 'grabbing hand' purposes. The 'grabbing hand' of lower-level bureaucrats should be viewed as a consequence, however, rather than the cause of the distortions and regulations created by the first-generation leaders, who did not have much personal motivation other than the dream of nation building. Similarly, various interest groups may also subsequently take advantage of these interventions/regulations and seek rents to benefit themselves. The vested-interest group's rent seeking was an unintended consequence, however, unrelated to the first-generation leaders' motivation for the interventions/regulations.

[9] The importance of ideas in determining the institutions is also emphasised by Lal (1994), Lal and Myint (1996) and North (1996).

as predicted by Schultz. The dominant social thought about the approach for successful transition in the 1980s and 1990s was, however, again based on an incorrect understanding of the underlying causes of poor performance and constraints on developing countries. Apart from a few countries, such as China and Vietnam – whose governments were not influenced by the dominant social thought at that time – most developing countries, both socialist and non-socialist, encountered severe setbacks in their economies during the transition process.[10]

In the following chapters, I analyse why the dominant social thought about developing countries' modernisation in the 1950s and 1960s and about transition in the 1980s and 1990s was incorrect, and how it shaped government policies and the established institutions in developing countries. I also discuss why the governments of a few economies in east Asia escaped the influence of the dominant social thinking in the 1950s and 1960s, and why China and Vietnam did not follow the transitional approach advocated by the prevailing social thought of the 1980s and 1990s.

---

[10] If the propositions of Olson (1982), Acemoglu, Johnson and Robinson (2001, 2002, 2005) and Engerman and Sokoloff (1997) are valid, the destiny of a nation depends on its history. As argued by Lewis (1955: 418), however, 'If we ask why a people has made a certain choice, the answer lies usually in its history; but if we ask why it has had that particular history, we are back among the mysteries of the universe. Fortunately, not all the answers depend upon history.' According to my proposition, the destiny of a nation can change. When the leadership in a country follows a new, right idea and adopts new policies, it can unleash dynamic growth.

THREE

Aspirations and social thought
of modernisation

Without the establishment of heavy industries in China, there can be no solid national defense, no well-being for the people, no prosperity and strength for the nation.

Mao Zedong (1945)

No country can be politically and economically independent, even within the framework of international interdependence, unless it is highly industrialized and has developed its power resources to the utmost.

Jawaharlal Nehru (1946)

Keynes (1926: 16) writes, '[A] study of the history of opinion is a necessary preliminary to the emancipation of the mind.' In this chapter, I review the evolution of social thought regarding the role of the government in the industrialisation and transition of developing countries.

Before the Industrial Revolution in the eighteenth century, China was more industrialised than the West (Cipolla, 1980; Elvin, 1973; Jones, 1981; Needham, 1969). In the seventeenth century the Indian subcontinent was not significantly less developed than Britain and, before 1800, India was a major supplier of cotton and silk textiles in international markets, including to Europe (Dutt, 1992). After the Industrial Revolution in Britain in the mid-eighteenth century, and in western Europe in the nineteenth century, the West was quickly industrialised and enhanced its economic, military and political power to achieve a dominant position in the world – hence the great divergence between the industrialised North and the agrarian South emerged. India, like many other parts of the world, became a colony. China was defeated repeatedly by the industrialised powers after the Opium War in 1840 and became a quasi-colony, ceding extraterritorial rights in treaty ports to twenty foreign countries; its customs revenues were controlled by foreigners, and it surrendered territory to Britain, Japan and Russia. Like the citizens of China and India, people in most other parts of the developing world were unable to control their own fate; their economies were plundered and exploited by the colonisers.

After the First World War nationalism became a popular trend, and after the Second World War most colonies became independent, led by veteran leaders of the various independence movements. The emergence of previous colonies or semi-colonies as newly independent states in Asia and the Middle East, and later in Africa, was accompanied by strong nationalist sentiments. Compared with developed countries, these developing countries had an extremely low economic growth rate and per capita gross national product (GNP), high birth and death rates, low average educational attainments and very little infrastructure. They were heavily specialised in the production and export of primary commodities and imported most of their manufactured goods. Thus, it was central to every developing government's national agenda to develop its economy independently so as to achieve a rapid economic take-off and eliminate poverty. As such, many developing country governments regarded economic growth as their direct and prime responsibility.

The lack of industrialisation – especially the possession of large heavy industries, which were the basis of military strength and economic power – had forced China, India and other areas in the developing world to yield to the colonial powers. It was natural, therefore that there emerged the social thinking of prioritising the development of large, advanced, heavy industrial sectors as a pre-requisite of modernisation, and the political and social elites in the developing world followed this social thought for their attempts at nation building after they had gained political independence from colonial rule (Lal and Myint, 1996: chap. 7).

In effect, the political leaders in Germany, France and other countries in western Europe in the nineteenth century pursued exactly the same goal when they saw the contrasts between the United Kingdom's rising industrial power and the backwardness of their own predominately agrarian economies (Gerschenkron, 1962). The desire to develop heavy industries also existed in the minds of revolutionary leaders from the very beginning of political movements in the developing world. Dr Sun Yat-sen, the father of modern China, proposed the development of 'key and basic industries' as a priority in his plan for China's industrialisation in 1919 (Sun, 1929).[1] Similarly, before the success of the socialist revolution, in a meeting in 1944 Mao Zedong, the leader of the Communist Party of China (CPC), advocated:

> [T]he reason for China's backwardness is mainly the lack of modern industry. [...] Therefore to eliminate this kind of backwardness is the mission of our entire nation. The common people support the Communist Party because we represent the demands of the nation and the people. However, if we cannot resolve economic problems, if we cannot build modern industry, and if we cannot develop productive power, then the common people will not necessarily support us. (Mao, 1944 [1978])

---

[1] Understanding the lack of capital in China, Dr Sun planned to borrow foreign capital for China's industrialisation. His position was different from Mao's and many other revolutionary leaders in China and in other developing countries, who advocated the idea of self-reliance.

Zhou Enlai – the prime minister after the founding of the People's Republic of China and an intimate associate of Mao – also quoted Mao in a speech given in 1953:

> [C]hairman Mao once said: our nation has obtained political independence, but if our nation wants to achieve complete independence, the completion of industrialisation is necessary. If the industry is not developed, a country may become the other country's vassal even after the country has obtained independence. As a socialist country, can we have a dependence mentality? For example, let the USSR develop heavy industries and national defence industries and let our nation develop light industries. Can we do that? In my opinion, we cannot do that. (Zhou, 1953 [1984]: 253; author's translation)

The Communist Party won the revolution and founded the People's Republic of China in 1949. After three years of recovery from the civil war China started its first five-year plan in 1953 under the leadership of Mao. The purpose of the plan was expressed explicitly as '[c]oncentrating the nation's efforts on industrial development with heavy industries as the core in order to build up the primary base of socialist industrialization' (CPC, 1955: 160–1). In 1957 Mao further proposed to make China's level of industrialisation exceed that of the United Kingdom in ten years and to catch up with that of the United States in fifteen years (Teiwes with Sun, 1999).

Similarly, the leadership of the freedom movement in India pressed hard for industrial development, even while the political struggle was going on. The Congress Party established a National Planning Committee to chart industrial development nearly a decade before India became independent, in 1947 (Dhar, 2003). In a speech, Jawaharlal Nehru – India's leader in the independence movement and the country's first prime minister – proclaimed:

> [N]o modern nation can exist without certain essential articles which can be produced only by big industry. Not to produce these is to rely on imports from abroad and thus to be subservient to the economy of

foreign countries ... Big industry must be encouraged and developed as rapidly as possible, but the type of industry thus encouraged should be chosen with care. It should be heavy and basic industry, which is the foundation of a nation's economic strength and on which other industries can gradually be built up. (cited in Srinivasan, 1994)

Under the leadership of Nehru, therefore, the Indian government's industrial policy resolutions of 1948 and 1956 entrusted the public sector with the responsibility for developing basic and heavy industry, and saw such development as a precondition for the development and expansion of the private sector (Dutt and Sundharam, 2006). With the assistance of Professor Prasanta Mahalanobis, India began to pursue the development of basic and heavy machine-building industries in its second five-year plan, which began in 1956.

In Latin America, political leaders and social elites were influenced strongly by the deterioration in the terms of trade, the economic difficulty encountered during the Great Depression in the 1930s and the thesis developed by Prebisch (1950) and Singer (1950). They believed that the decline in the terms of trade against the export of primary commodities was secular, which resulted in the transfer of income from resource-intensive developing countries to capital-intensive developed countries. They argued that the way for a developing country to avoid being exploited by developed countries was to develop domestic manufacturing industries through a process known as import substitution.

The thought of prioritising the development of heavy industry in developing countries also drew on the intellectual support of the writings of Marx and Lenin, and the Soviet Union's successful experience of industrialisation before the Second World War. In *Das Kapital*, Marx – based on Quesnay's *Tableau Economique* (1758–59)[2] – used a two-sector model, in which the first sector produced the

---

[2] For an authoritative compilation of the various editions of the *Tableau*, see Kuczynsky and Meek (1972).

means of production (that is, heavy industry) and the second sector produced consumer goods (that is, light industry and agriculture), to study the reproduction process. In the analysis, Marx argued that the means-of-production sector should grow more rapidly than the consumption goods sector in the modern production mode.

Following Marx, Lenin stressed the needs to prioritise the development of large-scale heavy industry in a frequently cited article entitled 'On the So-called Question of the Market', written in 1893. The position was reaffirmed in 'The Immediate Tasks of the Soviet Government', written after the Bolshevik Revolution (Lenin, 1918 [1972]), in which Lenin said, '[T]he raising of the productivity of labour first of all requires that the material basis of large-scale industry shall be assured, namely, the development of the production of fuel, iron, the engineering and chemical industries.' Because of the chaos and destruction from the civil war (1918–20) immediately following the Russian Revolution, however, Lenin was unable to put into practice the prioritisation of heavy industry development, and instead adopted the New Economic Policy (NEP) in 1921 to restore the shattered agricultural economy. After succeeding Lenin and consolidating his power, Stalin started to pursue earnestly the prioritised development of heavy industries in 1929 through a series of five-year plans (Gregory and Harrison, 2005; Gregory and Stuart, 2001). The share of heavy industry in Soviet industrial output rose rapidly (Allen, 2003; Moravcik, 1965) and the Soviet Union quickly became a global military power before the Second World War.[3]

---

[3] In 1929 the Great Depression began in the West. During the 1930s economic development in the West was beset with crises and stagnation. Led by Stalin, the Soviet Union adopted a planned economic system and prioritised the development of heavy industries. As the country with the most abundant natural resources per capita in the world, it had great potential to sustain its investment-led growth by mobilising natural resources to support investment. By the Second World War, the Soviet Union had already become industrialised, with strong military industries. The disadvantages of the planned economy were not revealed until the 1970s. The sharp contrast in economic performance between the Soviet Union and the developed capitalist countries in the 1930s had a profound impact on the thinking and policies

Running parallel to the political aspiration for heavy industry development in developing countries, there was a dominant view of 'market failure' in academic circles. The view held that, due to structural rigidities and coordination problems in the market in a developing country, heavy industries were unable to develop spontaneously. The market failure thesis became the core of the 'development economics' that emerged after the Second World War.[4] Under the influence of Keynesianism and the belief in the economic success of the Soviet Union, mainstream theories in the early phase of development economics argued that the market encompassed insurmountable defects and the government was a powerful supplementary means to accelerate the pace of economic development. Many development economists at that time advocated that the government should play a leading role in the industrialisation push, directly allocating the resources for investment, and setting up public enterprises in the large heavy industries to control the 'commanding heights' in order to overcome market failures (Hirschman, 1958; Nurkse, 1953; Rosenstein-Rodan, 1943).

The thought that the government in a lagging country needs to support the manufacturing industry in order to catch up with developed countries can be traced to the writings of List (1841

Footnote no. 3 (cont.)

    of social elites and political leaders in the developing world after the Second World War.

  [4] The new field of development economics was regarded as covering underdevelopment because 'conventional economics' did not apply (Hirschman, 1982). Early trade and development theories and policy prescriptions were based on some widely accepted stylised facts and premises about developing countries (Krueger, 1997); these included: (i) developing economies' production structures were oriented heavily towards primary commodity production; (ii) if developing countries adopted policies of free trade, their comparative advantage would lie for ever in primary commodity production; (iii) the global income elasticity and the price elasticity of demand for primary commodities were low; and (iv) capital accumulation was crucial for growth, and, in the early stages of development, it could occur only with the importation of capital goods. Based on these stylised facts and premises, it was a straight step to believe that the process of development was industrialisation, and industrialisation consisted primarily of the substitution of domestic production of manufactured goods for imports (Chenery, 1958).

[1910]), the 'father' of the 'infant industry for protection' argument. He argued that each lagging nation should foster the development of its own manufactures by import duties and even outright prohibitions, and only by this means could countries such as Germany, Russia and the United States – which at that time were less developed than the United Kingdom – ever hope to compete on equal terms with the United Kingdom. After List's death in 1846, Otto von Bismarck – the prime minister of Germany's Second Reich – put the ideas List advocated into practice in 1879. Bismarck used protective tariffs and direct government support in the development of iron, steel and other major heavy industries and turned Germany from a somewhat less developed agrarian economy into a major industrialised power in a short time. List's thesis and Germany's industrialisation experience impressed social elites and national leaders in India and other parts of the developing world, and shaped their thinking about the government's role and industrial policies in their national development – even to this day (Dhar, 2003).

Lal (1983) calls List's policy recommendations and the early development economics '*dirigiste* dogma'. Based on the teachings of development economics at that time, the international development agencies that were established after the Second World War – such as the World Bank, the IMF and the United Nations Commission for Trade and Development (UNCTAD) – enthusiastically advised the governments in developing countries to play an active role in overcoming market failures in their industrial development.

Aspirations and social thought have consequences. After the Second World War most developing countries – including socialist and non-socialist countries in Asia, Latin America and Africa – adopted a development strategy that prioritised large, advanced, capital-intensive industries (referred to commonly as the heavy-industry-oriented development strategy or import substitution strategy) to ensure their nations' independence and modernisation, to achieve higher living standards for their people, and to avoid exploitation by developed countries. They hoped that this strategy would help to establish an industrial system that was similar to those in developed countries. I argue in the next chapter, however, that it is incorrect to refer to the lack of the spontaneous development of heavy industry in a developing country as a market failure. Advanced capital-intensive heavy industry does not fit with the comparative advantages of developing countries; firms in heavy industries will not be viable in undistorted, open, competitive markets. It is primarily the viability problem – and not market rigidities or coordination failures – that resulted in the lack of large, advanced, capital-intensive industry in developing countries. I show that, due to this incorrect diagnosis, government policies based on the dominant social thought at the time resulted in pervasive government failures in developing countries, which have been discussed extensively by Bauer (1984), Krueger (1990) and Lal (1983) – to name just a few.

FOUR

Development strategy, viability and performance

The key characteristics of the endowment structure[1] in developing countries are a relative abundance of natural resources or unskilled labour and a scarcity of human and physical capital. In developing countries with abundant unskilled labour or resources but scarce human and physical capital, only the labour-intensive and resource-intensive industries will have comparative advantages in open, competitive markets; and in developed countries with abundant capital and relatively scarce labour, capital-intensive industries will be the most competitive[2] (Heckscher and Ohlin, 1991; Lin, 2003; Lin and Zhang, 2007; Ohlin, 1967). The development strategy advocated by

[1] 'Endowment structure' refers to the relative abundance of capital, labour and natural resources.

[2] The principle of comparative advantage – based on different labour productivity – has its origin in the works of David Ricardo, J. S. Mill and Alfred Marshall. The modern version of comparative advantage proposed by Heckscher and Ohlin (1991) is based on comparative costs, due to differences in the factor endowment structure. I draw inspiration from Heckscher and Ohlin (1991) in developing my arguments. In their model, however, the technology in each industry is assumed to be identical in the developed and developing countries, and a country is supposed to produce more goods that use its abundant factor intensively to exchange for goods that use its scarce factor intensively. More realistically, however, the technologies used in the developed and developing countries are not identical. Lin and Zhang (2007) build a dynamic model to show that a country should go into the industries and adopt the technologies that use its abundant factor intensively to produce goods. Their

the dominant social thought in development economics in the 1950s and 1960s and pursued by governments in many developing countries after the Second World War was, in essence, a comparative-advantage-defying (CAD) strategy.

4.1 CAD strategy, viability and endogenous distortions

Under a CAD strategy, firms in prioritised industries cannot survive in an open, competitive market because they are in conflict with the comparative advantages determined by their endowment structure and will require higher costs to produce goods than firms in countries with a comparative advantage in the same industries. Even if they are well managed, they cannot earn a socially acceptable profit in an undistorted, open, competitive market. I refer to these firms as non-viable.[3] In other words, these non-viable enterprises are unable to survive in an open, competitive market even if they are well managed; and, unless the government provides subsidies and/or protection, no one will invest in or continue to operate such firms. The lack of capital-intensive industries in developing countries is not, therefore, due to market rigidity but to the non-viability of the firms in an undistorted, open, competitive market.[4]

Footnote no. 2 (*cont.*)

 model allows a country to move up its technology and industry ladders along with the upgrading of its endowment structure from relative scarcity in capital to relative abundance in capital. Based on that model, I show in this book that a country's optimal industry/technology choice is endogenously determined by its endowment structure at each stage of its economic development and the optimal industry/technology choice should be upgraded according to the accumulation of capital in the endowments.

[3] If a normally managed firm is expected to earn a socially acceptable profit in a free, competitive market without government protection or subsidies, the firm is viable. There could be many factors that affect the viability of a firm. In this book, as well as in my other work, I use the term 'non-viability' to describe the inability of normally managed firms to earn socially acceptable profits due to their choices of industry, product and technology being at variance with those deemed optimal by the economy's endowment structure.

[4] The models based on increasing returns, such as Krugman (1981, 1987, 1991) and Matsuyama (1991), and in the coordination of investments, such as Murphy, Shleifer and Vishny (1989), assume that the endowment structure of each country

As I show in the mathematic model in appendix 1, in order to implement a CAD strategy a developing country government has to protect numerous non-viable enterprises; because these governments usually have limited tax collection capacities, however, such large-scale protection and subsidies cannot be sustained with their limited fiscal resources. The government has to resort to administrative measures – granting the non-viable enterprises in prioritised industries a market monopoly, suppressing interest rates,[5] overvaluing domestic currency and controlling prices for raw materials – to reduce the investment and operation costs of the non-viable enterprises. Such intervention will cause widespread shortages in funds, foreign exchange and raw materials. The government, therefore, needs to allocate these resources directly to these enterprises through administrative channels, including national planning in the socialist countries and credit rationing, investment and entry licensing in non-socialist developing countries.[6]

4.2 CAD strategy and its consequences

Although, with the above administrative measures, a developing country can build up industries that are in conflict with the

is identical, and, therefore, that firms will be viable in an undistorted, open, competitive market once the government helps the firms overcome market failure and escape the poor equilibrium trap. Such models could be appropriate for considering the government's role in assisting firms to compete with those in other countries in a similar stage of development. Such models are inappropriate as policy guidance for developing countries that are attempting to catch up with developed countries, however, because the endowment structures in developing and developed countries are different. With government help, a developing country might be able to set up firms in advanced capital-intensive industries that have economies of scale; because of the scarcity of human and physical capital, however, the comparative cost of production of firms in the industry in the developing country will be higher than for firms in a developed country in the same industry. The firms will, therefore, still be non-viable in an undistorted, open, competitive market. As such, the government needs to support and protect the firms continuously after they have been set up.

[5] The financial repression discussed by McKinnon (1973) and Shaw (1973) is a result of this strategy.

[6] The excessive regulation and administrative control will cause many private activities to escape into informal sectors (de Soto, 1987).

comparative advantage of the economy, serious information problems arise. Under information asymmetry, because the government cannot participate directly in the management of firms, it is impossible to determine the necessary amount of protection and subsidisation. When an enterprise incurs a loss, therefore – even if it is due to mismanagement or moral hazard problems on the part of managers – the blame will fall on the government for insufficient protection and subsidies, and the enterprise will use this as an excuse to ask for even more protection and subsidies. When the government is responsible for the losses of such enterprises, 'soft budget constraint' problems will arise (Lin and Tan, 1999)[7] and rent-seeking behaviour will be pervasive (Krueger, 1974). It is also inevitable that some government officials will use their power to intervene with the management of the enterprises and elicit bribery when the government needs to protect and subsidise the enterprises repeatedly.

After the adoption of a CAD strategy, in addition to the problems discussed above, a developing country might no longer benefit from the advantage of backwardness. It can no longer borrow technology from developed countries to accelerate its technological innovation and upgrade its industrial structure, because the development of new technology – either through independent research or foreign borrowing – requires capital investment. Under a CAD strategy, because limited capital resources are used to develop prioritised capital-intensive industries, labour-intensive industries that have comparative advantages cannot receive sufficient financial support and have to rely on traditional technologies. Firms in prioritised industries are unable to produce an economic surplus due to the violation

---

[7] The 'soft budget constraint' is a term coined by Kornai (1986), which became a popular research subject after the article by Dewatripont and Maskin (1995). According to Kornai, the soft budget constraint is a result of the paternalism of a socialist state; and, according to Dewatripont and Maskin, it is an endogenous phenomenon, arising from a time inconsistency problem. In Lin and Tan (1999) and Lin and Li (2008), I argue that the soft budget constraint arises from the policy burdens imposed on enterprises.

of comparative advantage.[8] Firms in industries consistent with the economy's comparative advantage will produce fewer surpluses than they could otherwise produce because of their difficulty in accessing the necessary capital for investment. Therefore, little economic surplus is generated and the surplus available for investment in the next period is limited. Due to patent protections and embargoes on advanced technology from developed countries, it will be difficult to borrow new advances at low cost in advanced industries. At the same time, independent research and development will require too much capital investment and involve too much risk. With an overall poor economic performance and limited surplus, the ability to carry out such research will inevitably fall short. After a few years these once advanced industries will become obsolete. As a result, technological progress in prioritised industries and the whole economy will be very slow and the technology gap with developed countries will soon widen.

A CAD strategy will also affect income distribution. In socialist countries that have eliminated capitalists, the development of prioritised industries can be realised through direct government investment, accompanied by the suppression and equalisation of wage rates through administrative measures. The equality is artificial. In other market-based countries, however, income distribution will be polarised (Lin and Chen, 2007; Lin and Liu, 2008). In these countries, only wealthy and/or crony capitalists, who have intimate relationships with the government and opportunities to access bank loans and fiscal resources, have the ability to invest in prioritised capital-intensive industries. Since subsidies to prioritised industries have to come from those workers and peasants who are relatively poor and unable to invest in the prioritised industries through direct or indirect taxations, the adoption of a CAD strategy will inevitably

[8] With the government's protection and subsidies, firms in the prioritised industries might appear to be very profitable. These profits, however, come from the transfer of surplus from other industries through the government's administrative measures, such as a price scissor between industry and agriculture (Sah and Stiglitz, 1984, 1987a). Such profits do not constitute a 'real' economic surplus in the economy.

polarise income distribution. Meanwhile, because the prioritised industries are capital-intensive, they can generate only limited employment opportunities. The labour-intensive industries that could generate more employment opportunities cannot develop fully due to the lack of capital. As a result, large numbers of labourers are either retained in rural areas or become unemployed or semi-employed. As such, the wage rate is repressed. Therefore, even if fast investment-led growth is achieved at the beginning, the poor will not benefit from the growth (Lal and Myint, 1996).

In summary, while the adoption of a CAD strategy can establish some advanced industries in developing countries, it inevitably leads to inefficient resource allocation, suppressed working incentives, rampant rent-seeking behaviour, deteriorating income distribution and poor economic performance. In the end: more haste, less speed. The adoption of a CAD strategy will not narrow the gap between developing and developed countries; instead, the gap will become wider and wider.[9]

4.3 CAF strategy, competitive markets and a facilitating state

What political leaders and social elites fail to recognise is the fact that the industrial and technological structures in developed coun-

---

[9] In the models of Acemoglu, Johnson and Robinson (2001, 2002, 2005), Engerman and Sokoloff (1997), Grossman and Helpman (1996, 2001) and Olson (1982), government intervention, institutional distortions and rent seeking arise from the capture of government by powerful vested-interest elites. Logically, their models can explain some observed interventions and distortions, such as import quotas, tax subsidies, entry regulations and so on. Their theories cannot, however, explain the existence of other important interventions and distortions – for example, the pervasiveness of public-owned enterprises in developing countries, which are against the interests of the powerful elites. Appendix 1 provides a formal model for the observed set of seemingly unrelated or even self-conflicting distortions and interventions in developing countries based on the need to support non-viable firms arising from the conflicts between the CAD strategy pursued by the government and the given endowment structure in the economy. Once the government introduces a distortion, however, a group of vested interests will be created even if the distortion is created for noble purpose. The vested-interest argument could be appropriate for explaining the difficulty of removing distortions.

tries are determined endogenously by their economic endowment structures. Without government interventions, industries in developing countries are more labour- and resource-intensive because human and physical capital is relatively scarce and labour and resources are relatively abundant. Since industrial and technological structures are endogenous to the endowment structure of the economy, the goal of a government's development strategy should be to upgrade the endowment structure, instead of upgrading industry and technology directly without taking measures to upgrade the endowment structure first.[10] Once the endowment structure is upgraded, relative factor prices will change and the profit motive and competition pressures will force enterprises to upgrade their industrial and technological structures spontaneously.

Upgrading the endowment structure requires capital to accumulate more rapidly than the growth of labour and natural resources; this applies to material capital and human capital. Capital accumulation depends on the total economic surplus and savings in the economy. If the development of industries and the adoption of technology in a developing country follow the comparative advantage determined by its endowment structure at every phase of development, then industries will be most competitive in domestic and world markets at all times.[11] As a result, products will acquire the largest possible market share and generate the largest possible surplus. Since the capital investment has acquired the largest possible return, the returns on savings will also be the highest possible.

---

[10] It is a general principle that the government will create distortions if it aims to change an endogenous phenomenon directly without changing the underlying conditions/ constraints that cause the phenomenon to exist.

[11] Porter (1990) has made the term 'competitive advantage' popular. According to him, nations will have competitive advantage in the global economy if they fulfil the following four conditions: (i) their industries intensively use the nationally abundant and relatively inexpensive factors of production; (ii) their products have large domestic markets; (iii) each industry forms domestic clusters; and (iv) markets are competitive. The first condition means in effect that an economy's industrial comparative advantage should be determined by the nation's endowments. The third and the

Consequently, households will have the highest savings propensity, resulting in the fastest possible upgrade of the endowment structure. I refer to the set of policies that facilitates the development of industries and the adoption of technology in a developing country to follow the comparative advantage determined by its endowment structure at every phase of development as a comparative-advantage-following (CAF) strategy.

An enterprise's choices of industry and technology depend on the relative prices of capital, labour and natural resources. Only when relative prices fully reflect the relative scarcity of these production factors will the enterprise's choices be consistent with the comparative advantage determined by the endowment structure. This requires that the product and factor markets be fully competitive. Since markets in developing countries are usually not fully competitive, the adoption of a CAF strategy requires the government to improve various market institutions so as to create and protect effective competition in the product and factor markets – as advocated by Smith (1776 [1976]), Marshall (1920) and, more recently, Bauer (1984), Lal (1983) and Little (1982).

The government in a developing country could, however, play a more active role to facilitate economic development than just maintaining market competition, as advocated by proponents of minimum government. When the government in a developing country follows a CAF strategy, and as capital accumulates, the endowment structure will upgrade, causing relative factor prices to change. Enterprises need to upgrade their industries and technologies accordingly in order to maintain market competitiveness. In the

Footnote no. 11 (*cont.*)
fourth conditions will hold only if the industries are consistent with the nation's competitive advantage. Therefore, the four conditions can be reduced to independent conditions: the comparative advantage and domestic market size. Among these two independent conditions, the comparative advantage is more important than the domestic market size, because if an industry is the nation's comparative advantage the industry's product will have a global market. This is the reason why, among the richest countries in the world, many of them are very small (Lin and Ren, 2007).

process, enterprises in developing countries can benefit from the industrial and technological gap with developed countries by acquiring industrial and technological innovations that are consistent with their new comparative advantage through learning and borrowing from developed countries. In particular, they can borrow technologies from those countries whose stage of development is higher than but not too far away from theirs.[12] Compared with innovation through independent research in developed countries, such acquisition of innovation has a lower cost and less risk. The speed of technological innovation will therefore be faster in the developing country that adopts a CAF strategy than in the developed country.[13]

In the above discussions, I assume that information about the product markets, industries and production technologies are available

[12] This is one of the most important principles for the successful application of the advantage of backwardness. Historically, for those countries relying successfully on the advantage of backwardness to achieve industrialisation – that is, the continental countries in western Europe in the nineteenth century and the east Asian NIEs after the Second World War – they all borrowed technology from countries whose per capita income was not too much greater than theirs. In such circumstances, the borrowed technology will be consistent with the borrowing country's comparative advantage, and the enterprises using the borrowed technology will be viable. According to the estimations of Maddison (2006), the per capita incomes of the continental countries in western Europe were about 60 per cent of that of the United Kingdom in 1870. Similarly, in post-war development, the four NIEs borrowed technology from Japan instead of North America and western Europe. In addition, the technology and industry transferred from Japan to the NIEs followed a flying goose pattern in the initial stages (Akamatsu, 1962) – that is, industrial development in the east Asian NIEs followed one step behind the Japanese industries (Kim, 1988). For the poorer countries in eastern Europe – such as Hungary and Russia – whose per capita income was about 30 per cent of that of the United Kingdom in 1870, an attempt similar to that by western European countries in the late nineteenth century resulted in a much higher degree of government intervention and direct involvement, causing various difficulties and economic stagnation after the industries were established (Gerschenkron, 1962). When borrowing technology from advanced countries, however, developing countries often aim for the most advanced technology, causing all kinds of difficulties due to the CAD nature of such borrowing.

[13] The above discussion does not mean that a country that follows a CAF strategy does not need to engage in indigenous innovation. To be successful, the country needs to undertake process innovation to make the borrowed technology suitable to local conditions. The country also needs to do indigenous product innovation in sectors in which the country has already been the world leader or has been just a step behind the world leader. For further discussions, see Lin and Ren (2007).

freely to the firms in the economy.[14] When the factor endowment structure of the economy is upgraded, therefore, enterprises can upgrade their technologies or upgrade smoothly from less capital-intensive industry to somewhat more capital-intensive industry. Such information might not be available, however; therefore, it is necessary to invest resources to search for, collect and analyse the industry, product and technology information. If an enterprise carries out the activities on its own, it will keep the information private, and other enterprises will be required to make the same investment to obtain the information. There will be repetition in the information investment. The information does have a public goods aspect, however. After the information has been gathered and processed, the cost of its dissemination is close to zero. The government can, therefore, collect the information about the new industries, markets and technology and make it available to all firms in the form of an industrial policy.

The upgrading of technology and industry often requires the coordination of different enterprises and sectors in the economy. For example, the human capital or skill requirements of new industries/technologies might be different from those used with older industries/technologies. An enterprise may not be able to internalise the supply of the new requirements and may need to rely on outside sources; therefore, the success of a firm's industry/technology upgrade depends also on the existence of an outside supply of new human capital. In addition to human capital, firms that are upgrading might require support for new financial institutions, trading arrangements, marketing and distribution facilities, intellectual property rights protection and so on. A government might, therefore, also use industrial policy to coordinate firms in different industries and sectors for the upgrading of industry/technology in the economy.[15] Developing

---

[14] The next six paragraphs, on the government's role in overcoming information, coordination and externality issues, are drawn from Lin (2003).

[15] Most 'big push' attempts by the less developed countries (LDCs) in the 1950s and 1960s failed. There has been renewed interest in the idea, however, since the influential article by Murphy, Shleifer and Vishny (1989). Their paper showed that gov-

countries generally lag behind in their infrastructure, financial institutions, legal systems and other social development, so a government should also invest in infrastructure and strengthen the development of legal, financial and social institutions along with the industrial upgrading.[16] A government also needs to build up its administrative capacity in order to carry out the above functions.

The upgrading of industry/technology is an innovation, and it is risky by nature. Even with the information and coordination provided by a government's industry policy, an enterprise's attempt to upgrade its industry/technology might fail due to the upgrade being too ambitious, the new market being too small, the coordination being simply inadequate and so on. The failure will indicate to other firms that the targets of the industrial policy are inappropriate, and, therefore, that they can avoid such failure by not following the policy. In other words, the first enterprise pays the cost of failure and provides valuable information for other enterprises. If the first enterprise succeeds, the success will also provide information externalities to other enterprises, prompting them to engage in similar upgrades.

ernment coordination and support were required for setting up a key industry and that the demand spillovers from the key industry to other industries would enhance economic growth. For the big push strategy to be successful, the 'pushed' industry must be consistent with the comparative advantage – which is determined by the relative factor endowment of the economy – and the firms in the pushed industry must be viable after the push. Deviation from comparative advantage in the pushed industries and the consequent lack of viability of the chosen firms are the reasons why so many big push attempts by LDCs in the 1950s and 1960s failed.

16 For example, the optimal financial institution will be different in a country at an early agrarian stage of development from one is a modern, industrialised stage of development, and the government needs to play an active role to facilitate the transition from and operation of one institution to another institution along the development path. At the early agrarian stage most financial transactions are between rich landlords and poor tenant farmers. The dominant form of financial arrangement is informal. Transactions rely mainly on private enforcement to prevent the problem of moral hazards. With the coming and deepening of industrialisation, the demands for capital increase continuously, as well as the risk of investment. Formal financial arrangements, such as banks, bonds and equity markets, play an increasingly important role for mobilising financial resources and for sharing risks. The government needs to provide adequate regulation and supervision for the proper functioning of the above formal financial institutions.

These subsequent upgrades will dissipate the possible rents that the first enterprise might enjoy, so there is an asymmetry between the costs of failure and the gains of success that the pioneer enterprise might have. To compensate for the externality and the asymmetry between the possible costs and gains, the government could provide some form of subsidy – such as tax incentives or loan guarantees – to enterprises that initially follow the government's industrial policy.

As many studies of the success stories of the east Asian NIEs suggest, it is therefore desirable for a government to have an industrial policy to overcome the information, coordination and externality problems that are unavoidable in the process of development (Amsden, 1989; Chang, 1994; Wade, 1990).

Most developing countries lag behind developed countries not only in industry and technology but also in legal, financial and social institutions and state capacity. As the economy grows and per capita income increases, the economic and social transactions become increasingly complicated. In addition to overcoming the information, coordination and externality problems in the industrial upgrading, therefore, it is imperative for the government in a developing country to play an active role in supporting the development of social, economic and political institutions during the modernisation process so as to maintain social harmony.

I refer to the government in a developing country that plays the above roles to facilitate the economy's development along its changing comparative advantages as a 'facilitating state' – that is, a state that creates an enabling institutional environment that facilitates firms in the economy to follow its comparative advantages at each stage of its development, and makes it easier for citizens to adapt to an increasingly industrialised, modern life.[17]

---

[17] The development state theory also advises the government in a developing country to play an active role in the development process. Based on their observation of east Asia's successful development experiences, the proponents of development state theory urge the government of a developing country to adopt industrial policy to promote selected

4.4 CAD versus CAF: comparisons of role of government, income distribution and openness

The government that adopts a CAF strategy and the government that adopts a CAD strategy will both use an industrial policy to support the development of certain industries and technology. It is worthwhile noting, however, that there is a fundamental difference between these two types of industrial policy. The promoted industry/technology in the CAF strategy is consistent with the comparative advantage determined by changes in the economy's factor endowments, whereas the priority industry/technology that the CAD strategy attempts to promote is not. The enterprises in the CAF strategy should therefore be viable after they are established with the government's help in information and coordination, and a small, limited subsidy should be enough to compensate for the externality issue. In contrast, enterprises in the priority sectors of a CAD strategy are not viable, and their survival depends on large, continuous policy favours and support from the government.[18]

industries and to use distorted interest to subsidise the development of those industries in the process of a country's economic development. The development state theory does not specify that the chosen industries should be consistent with the country's comparative advantages, however, while the facilitating state theory does so. Moreover, the term 'developmental state' could cause some confusion, because the government that adopts a CAD strategy also carries out similar interventions to those proposed by development state theory to support the development of selective industries. As Lewis (1955: 376) observes, '[G]overnments may fail either because they do too little, or because they do too much.' If the government in a developing country follows the teaching of minimum state and does not play an active role in the development of industry, markets and institutions – as required by a CAF strategy – it is doing too little. If, however, the government adopts a CAD strategy, it is doing too much. The government will become a *dirigiste* state, as criticised by Lal (1983, 1994). For a recent review of development state theory, see Fritz and Menocal (2007) and ten other articles in *Development Policy Review*, volume 25, number 5 (September 2007).

[18] The dynamic comparative advantage is another argument often used for the government's industrial policy and support to firms (Redding, 1999). In my framework, however, it can be seen clearly that the argument is valid only if the government's support is limited to overcoming information and coordination costs and the pioneering firm's externality to other firms. The industry should be consistent with the comparative advantage of the economy and the firms in the new industry should be viable, otherwise the firms will collapse once the government's support is removed. If

A comparison of the successes and failures of industrial policies for automobile production in Japan, South Korea, India and China is a good illustration of the differences between the CAF and CAD industrial policies. The automobile industry is a typical capital-intensive heavy industry. The development of an automobile industry is the dream of most developing countries. Japan adopted an industrial policy to promote its automobile industry in the mid-1960s and achieved great success. Japan's experience is often cited as a supporting argument by advocates of an industrial policy for heavy industries in developing countries. South Korea instituted an industrial policy for automobile production in the mid-1970s and has achieved a limited degree of success. The automobile industries in China and India were started in the 1950s, and in both countries continuous government protection was still required thirty years after their establishment (Maxcy, 1981). What can explain why similar industrial policies yielded success in one instance and failure in another? This will be clear once we compare the per capita income of these countries with the per capita income of the United States at the time when the former initiated their policies (table 4.1).

Per capita income is a good proxy for the relative abundance of capital and labour in an economy. Capital is abundant and wage rates are high in a high-income country; in a low-income country, the opposite is true. Table 4.1 indicates that, when Japan initiated its automobile production policy in the mid-1960s, its per capita income was more than 40 per cent of that in the United States. The automobile industry was the United States' main industry, but it was

Footnote no. 18 (*cont.*)
   not, the required lengthy support to the firms in the industries advocated by most dynamic comparative advantage theories will crowd out the resources available to other firms that *are* consistent with the competitive advantage of the economy, and slow economic growth and capital accumulation. The economy will therefore reach the stage targeted by the dynamic advantage policy later than an economy that follows a CAF strategy (Lin and Zhang, 2007).

TABLE 4.1 *Level of per capita income (1990 Geary–Khamis dollars)*

	United States	Japan	South Korea	India	China
1955	10,970	2,695	1,197	665	818
1965	14,017	5,771	1,578	785	945
1975	16,060	10,973	3,475	900	1,250

Source: Maddison (1995: 196–205).

not the most advanced, capital-intensive industry at that time nor was Japan a capital-scarce economy. The Ministry of International Trade and Industry (MITI) gave support only to Nissan and Toyota; more than ten firms – ignoring MITI's prompting not to enter the industry – also started automobile production and were successful, even though they did not receive any support from MITI. As these firms were successful in open, competitive markets even without government support, this evidence indicates that the Japanese automobile firms were viable. Further more, the upgrading of the automobile industry in the 1960s reflected the upgrading in Japan's endowment structure as a result of rapid capital accumulation from the successful development of labour-intensive industries, such as textiles and garments, and conventional industries, such as steel and shipbuilding, in the post-war period. As such, MITI's promotion of the automobile industry in the 1960s was consistent with the requirement of a CAF strategy.

When South Korea initiated its automobile industry development policy in the 1970s, however, its per capita income was only about 20 per cent of that of the United States and about 30 per cent of that of Japan. This could well explain why the South Korean government needed to give its automobile firms much greater and longer support than the Japanese government did. Even despite this support, two of the three automobile firms in South Korea fell into bankruptcy amid the east Asian financial crisis in the late 1990s. When China and India initiated their automobile industry development policies in the 1950s, their per capita incomes were less than 10 per cent of that of the United States. The automobile firms in China and India were not viable; therefore, their survival depended for a long time on heavy government protection.

Similarly, Bismarck's industrialisation push in the late nineteenth century did not result in Germany being caught in the Listian trap, but other less developed countries could not escape this fate when their governments adopted a similar set of policies to boost the development of capital-intensive heavy industries in central and eastern Europe in Bismarck's time, and in other parts of the developing world in the period after the Second World War (Hayami and Godo, 2005: chap. 8). As discussed in footnote 12, the difference is attributable to the fact that, in 1870, GDP per capita in Germany was $1,821 – measured in 1990 international dollars – which was 57 per cent of the United Kingdom's per capita GDP of $3,191 (Maddison, 2006: 264). Compared with the per capita income gap between the United States and the developing countries in the 1950s and 1960s and the gap between the United Kingdom (the most advanced country in the nineteenth century) and the central/east European countries in the late nineteenth century, the gap between Germany and the United Kingdom in Bismarck's time was relatively small. Bismarck's industrial policy was, therefore, consistent with the requirement of a CAF strategy.

Philosophically, the success of the iron and steel policies in Bismarck's Germany and the automobile industry policy in Japan in the 1960s, and the failure of industrial policies in most other developing countries, are good examples of the maxim that 'quantity difference leads to quality difference'. The industrial policies of Bismarck and Japan's MITI were an integral part of CAF strategies for the purposes of overcoming the information, coordination and externality problems arising from industrial upgrading, according to the requirements of changes in their factor endowments. The best proof is that, once the targeted industries were set up in Germany and Japan, their products could compete successfully in international markets without further government subsidies and protection. Although the industries targeted in other developing countries were similar to those in Germany and Japan, due to their low endowment structures their industrial policies were in the nature of a CAD strategy. Even after the industries were set up, their survival depended on continuous government protection and subsidies.

In short, a developing country government that plays the role of a facilitating state and adopts a CAF strategy needs, on the one hand, to build up and maintain competitive market institutions so that relative factor prices reflect the changes in the relative abundance of factor endowments in the economy and guide enterprises to make appropriate choices to upgrade industry and technology dynamically. On the other hand, the government needs actively to collect and disseminate technology/industry information plausibly in the form of industrial policy, coordinate the enterprises' investment, compensate for externalities and strengthen the legal, financial and social institutions in order to facilitate the enterprises' upgrading of industry and technology. If the developing country government plays the right facilitating roles, the country can benefit from the advantage of backwardness and be able to upgrade its endowment and industrial and technological structures more rapidly than a developed country. Lin and Zhang (2007) show that, in the end, the income level of this developing country will converge successfully with that of developed countries.[19]

Unlike the adoption of a CAD strategy – which will worsen income distribution, as discussed previously – the adoption of a CAF strategy can improve income distribution in the dynamic

---

[19] To implement the above functions, the government needs to have substantial state capacity; therefore, once the governments of countries such as India, China, Japan, Vietnam and the NIEs in east Asia change their ideas of development and perform the facilitating state's role, the countries can take off quickly. This could be the reason why Chanda and Putterman (2007) find that old states such as China and India have been experiencing more rapid economic growth in recent decades.

development process. When an economy's development is in its early stages, with relatively abundant labour and scarce capital, enterprises will initially enter labour-intensive industries and adopt more labour-intensive technologies. This will create as many employment opportunities as possible and will transfer labour from traditional sectors to modern manufacturing and service sectors. Accompanying the upgrading in the endowment structure, labour abundance will be replaced gradually with labour scarcity and capital scarcity will gradually become capital abundance. Accordingly, the cost of labour will increase and the cost of capital will decrease. Because capital income is the major source of income for the rich, while labour is the major source of income for the poor, such changes in relative prices will make it possible to achieve economic growth and equity simultaneously (Lin and Liu, 2008).[20]

Moreover, a country that follows a CAF strategy will be more outward-oriented than a country that follows a CAD strategy. The CAF country will develop and export goods in which it has comparative advantages and import the goods in which it does not have comparative advantages. In contrast, the CAD country will attempt to produce goods in which it does not have comparative advantages, and thus imports will be reduced; meanwhile, its exports will also be reduced, due to the relocation of resources away from sectors that are consistent with its comparative advantages, to sectors violating its comparative advantages. From the above comparison, the degree of openness to trade is endogenous to the government's development strategy. Therefore, the hypothesis that trade is a fundamental deter-

---

[20] The above argument does not belittle the government's role in achieving an equitable income distribution by income transfer and social protections. For example, the government needs to provide minimum living support to disabled and temporarily unemployed people as well as investing in education and vocational training to help labourers meet job requirements. If, however, all able-bodied labourers are employed, it will be much easier for the government to achieve an equitable society than otherwise. Moreover, such income transfer and social protections should be considered as secondary measures rather than as the primary means to achieve social equity.

minant of growth in a country could just reflect the fact that the successful countries are following their comparative advantages in their economic development.[21]

[21] The above discussion assumes that a country relies on its own capital for investment. The existence of international capital flow will not change the main conclusions. International capital could come to a developing country in two ways: by borrowing or direct investment. If the government borrows capital to invest in infrastructure or in industries that are consistent with the economy's comparative advantages, the capital inflow will benefit the economy's growth. If capital is borrowed to invest in sectors that are against comparative advantages – whether it is borrowed by the government or by the private sector – a period of investment-led growth could be prolonged, but the poor performance will not change and the economy could encounter crisis when it is time to repay the foreign debt. Foreign capital could come also as direct investment, for which there could be two possible purposes: to use the developing country as an export production base or to penetrate into the developing country's domestic markets. Investment for the former will be in sectors that are consistent with the country's comparative advantages; for the latter, the goods produced by the foreign-owned firms will be more advanced and capital-intensive than those produced by domestic firms. To reduce production costs, however, the foreign-owned firms will substitute the capital with low-cost local labour to the extent that the technology permits. Therefore, the capital intensity of the foreign subsidiary in a developing country will be lower than that in the home, developed country.

FIVE

Viability and strategies of transition

No matter whether it is a white cat or a black cat, as long as it can catch mice it is a good cat. The way to transit from a traditional planned economy to a market economy is just like crossing a river by groping for the stones beneath the surface.

Deng Xiaoping[1]

In a country that adopts a CAD strategy, it is likely that, in the early stages, the economy will enjoy a period of rapid investment-driven growth. As has been observed, however, in Latin America and many other developing and socialist countries, economic growth will inevitably slow down, leading to eventual stagnation and even frequent crises due to the low economic efficiency and consequent depletion of the economic surplus, which is required for investment, arising from the misallocation of resources, suppression of incentives, soft budget constraints and rent-seeking activities.

As predicted by the hypothesis of Schultz (1977) with regard to the interaction of social thinking and situations of economic and social development, the malfunctioning of established institutions in

---

[1] Deng Xiaoping (1904–97) was the leader who led China in its transition from a planned economy to a market economy from 1979 onwards by following a piecemeal, tinkering, gradualist approach without a blueprint for transition at the beginning.

the CAD strategy in turn alters the prevailing social thought about the role of government and of the market in economic development. Since the late 1970s a new form of social thought has arisen: Wiles (1995) has labelled it 'capitalist triumphalism' and its policies were encapsulated in the package of ten policy recommendations in the 'Washington Consensus' – a term coined by Williamson (1989).[2] The main idea of the Washington Consensus was to eliminate government interventions and distortions so as to create a private-property-based, efficient, open and competitive market economy. The 'shock therapy' that was advocated for eastern Europe and the former Soviet Union states for their transition to a market economy was a version of the Washington Consensus.

Economists are known for having diverse views on practically all issues, but, as Summers (1994) has written, when it comes to reforming a socialist economy there is a surprising consensus among mainstream economists for the adoption of shock therapy.[3] One element of shock therapy is the need for rapid privatisation. The arguments in support of this are as follows: private ownership is the foundation for a well-functioning market system; real market competition requires a real private sector (Sachs and Lipton, 1990); most problems encountered by state-owned enterprises in a transitional economy can be ameliorated by rapid privatisation (Sachs, 1992); and privatisation must take place before state-owned enterprises can

---

[2] The package of policies includes fiscal discipline, a redirection of public spending from indiscriminate subsidies towards the broad-based provision of pro-growth, poverty-alleviating services, broadening the tax base, interest rate liberalisation, a competitive exchange rate strategy, trade liberalisation, uniform tariffs, the liberalisation of inward foreign direct investment, the privatisation of state enterprises, the deregulation of market entry, prudent oversight of financial institution and legal protection of property rights.

[3] Certainly, a few economists have had dissenting views, Stiglitz being a notable example. In his book *Whither Socialism?*, Stiglitz (1994) questions the desirability of privatisation and other basic tenets of the Washington Consensus. Based on the theories of information asymmetry, Stiglitz argues that the government should play an active role to overcome market failures. Nonetheless, he does not distinguish between the role of a facilitating state for implementing a CAF strategy and that of a dirigiste state for implementing a CAD strategy.

be restructured (Blanchard *et al.*, 1991).[4] Another early consensus view for transition is the need for a total 'big-bang'-style price liberalisation. An influential article by Murphy, Shleifer and Vishny (1992) attributes the fall in outputs in the Soviet Union in 1990–1 to partial price liberalisation. They argue that a dual-track pricing system encouraged arbitrage, corruption, rent seeking and the diversion of scarce inputs from high-value to low-value use. The last element in shock therapy is the need to tighten a government's fiscal discipline to maintain macroeconomic stability so that prices can serve as a guide for resource allocation and the market mechanism can work effectively.

The three integral constituents of shock therapy – like the ten policy recommendations of the Washington Consensus – are logically consistent, and arguments in support of them are persuasive because the targets of such reforms are agreed to be the required institutional arrangements for a well-functioning market economy. Proponents expected that the simultaneous implementation of price liberalisation, rapid privatisation and fiscal discipline would allow countries to experience a 'J-curve' in their growth path – that is, a short-term transitional recession followed by a quick and dynamic growth rebound after the implementation of the package of reforms. As shown in figure 1.3, however, the transitional economies in eastern Europe and the former Soviet Union encountered deep recessions. For the eastern European economies, their per capita income levels did not recover until 2000 to the levels achieved before the transition in 1990; and, for the economies in the former

---

[4] There have been some economists arguing for an evolutionary, gradualist approach to privatisation in the transition. For example, Kornai (1990) argues that private property rights cannot be made to work by fiat in the transitional economies, where entire generations have been forced to forget the civic principles and values associated with private ownership and private rights, and become a mere imitation of the most refined legal and business forms of the leading capitalist countries. Kornai also believes, however, that private ownership is the foundation for a well-functioning market system and privatisation is the only way to eliminate state-owned enterprises' soft budget constraints.

Soviet Union, they have still not recovered to their pre-transition levels.[5] Other developing countries under the guidance of the IMF adopted the Washington Consensus package of reforms in the 1980s and 1990s, and their economic performances were also disappointing (Barro, 1998; Easterly, 2001a). Because of the failure of the Washington Consensus reforms to bring about rapid economic development and to eradicate poverty, there has been a resurgence of socialist ideology in Latin America in recent years, and some Latin American governments have decided to renationalise or to take majority shares in some privatised enterprises (Ishmael, 2007).

China, Vietnam and other east Asian transitional economies did not follow the Washington Consensus and adopted a dual-track, gradual approach – referred to by some economists as the 'Asian approach' (Chang and Noland, 1995; Rana and Hamid, 1995). In China, for example, instead of the rapid privatisation of its state-owned enterprises, the government continued its ownership of the enterprises and gave them subsidies through preferential access to subsidised credit. It also allowed private enterprises – including joint ventures – to enter the previously suppressed sectors (Perkins, 1998). This approach was once asserted to be the worst possible transition strategy, one that would invite rent seeking and corruption and result in unavoidable economic collapse (Sachs, Woo and Yang, 2000).[6] Likewise, most state-owned enterprises in Vietnam were not

---

[5] Slovenia is an exception in eastern Europe. It has enjoyed rapid growth in its transition to a market economy. Slovenia joined the European Union in May 2004 and the Eurozone on 1 January 2007. Slovenia did not, however, practise shock therapy. In addition to its excellent infrastructure, a well-educated workforce and an excellent central location, its privatisation did not gain momentum until 2002–5. Similarly, Poland – the other strong performer in eastern Europe – did not start to privatise its large state-owned enterprises until recently.

[6] Sachs and Woo (1994) attribute the remarkable growth rate during China's transition process to its large rural labour force, available to be reallocated to high-value manufacturing industries. Mongolia and many transitional economies in central Asia also have a large rural labour pool. Unlike China, however, they did not achieve a dynamic growth performance in the transitional process, but instead experienced a collapse similar to that in the more industrialised former Soviet states.

privatised and still enjoyed priority access to subsidised bank credits (Sun, 1997). Far from collapsing, however, China has been the most dynamic economy in the world in the past three decades. It has moved close to becoming a fully fledged market economy (Naughton, 1995) and achieving the ideal Pareto-improvement result of reform without losers (Lau, Qian and Roland, 2000; Lin, Cai and Li, 1996). Similarly, Vietnam's economy has been very dynamic since the start of its transition in the early 1980s.

Why did the Washington Consensus fail? Again, what went wrong was not the goal of setting up an open, competitive market system but the failure to recognise the endogenous nature of the distortions in the economic system before transition.

The objectives of the Washington Consensus reforms were to eliminate government distortions and interventions in socialist and developing countries, and to set up a well-functioning market system. If this goal is realised, market competition will determine the relative prices of various products and production factors, and relative prices will reflect their relative scarcities in factor endowments. Given these prices, market competition will induce enterprises to choose industries, products and technology that are consistent with the comparative advantages determined by the economy's endowment structure. Consequently, the economy will be able to make full utilisation of the advantage of backwardness, and will prosper.

What the Washington Consensus ignored, however, was that in countries that had adopted a CAD strategy there existed many non-viable enterprises. Without government protection and subsidies, those enterprises were unable to survive in an open and competitive market. If there were only a limited number of such non-viable enterprises, the output value and employment of those enterprises would be limited; shock therapy that eliminated all government interventions at once might be applicable. With the abolition of government protection and subsidies, these non-viable enterprises become bankrupt. The originally suppressed labour-intensive industries thrive, however, and newly created employment opportunities in these industries can surpass the losses from the bankruptcy of non-viable firms. As a result, the economy can grow dynamically soon after implementing the shock therapy, with at most a small loss of output and employment at the outset.

On the other hand, if the number of non-viable firms is too large, the output value and employment of those firms will make up too large a share in the national economy and shock therapy may be inapplicable. Its application will result in economic chaos due to large-scale bankruptcies and dramatic increases in unemployment. In order to avoid such dramatic increases in unemployment or to sustain these 'advanced' non-viable enterprises, the government has no choice but to continue its protection and subsidies for these firms, either explicitly or implicitly, in a more disguised way than the previous distortions – that is, changing the previous second best distortions to even worse third or fourth best distortions. Even if the firms are privatised, soft budget constraint problems will continue. The subsidies to the non-viable firms may even increase on account of the private owners having greater incentives to lobby for subsidies and protection (Lin and Li, 2008). In effect, this is what happened in Russia and many other countries in eastern Europe and the former Soviet Union (Brada, 1996; Frydman, Gary and Rapaczynski, 1996; Lavigne, 1995; Pleskovic, 1994; Stark, 1996; Sun, 1997; World Bank, 2002a). In the end, the economy can find itself in a problematic situation of shock without therapy (Kolodko, 2000).[7]

---

[7] The difference in the shares of non-viable firms in the economy might explain why the shock therapy recommended by Sachs succeeded in Bolivia but not in the economies of eastern Europe and the former Soviet Union. Bolivia is a poor, small economy; therefore, the resources that the government could mobilise to subsidise the non-viable firms were small and the share of non-viable firms in the economy was also relatively small. Stiglitz (1998) has questioned the universal applicability of the Washington Consensus. He points out that it advocated the use of a small set of instruments – including macroeconomic stability, liberalised trade and

Facing the endogenously formed distortions and the existence of large-scale non-viable enterprises in the economy, the dual-track gradual approach adopted by the Chinese government is arguably better than shock therapy (McKinnon, 1993). Instead of following the 'macro-institution first' approach proposed by the Washington Consensus, the Chinese government employed a 'micro first' approach to improve incentives for farmers and state-owned enterprise workers; it adopted the individual-household-based farming system to replace the collective farming system,[8] and introduced profit retention and managerial autonomy to state-owned enterprises,[9] making farmers and workers partial residual claimants. This reform greatly improved the incentives and productivity in agriculture and industry (Groves *et al.*, 1994; Jefferson and Rawski, 1995; Jefferson, Rawski and Zhang, 1992; Li, 1997; Lin, 1992;

Footnote no. 7 (*cont.*)

privatisation – to achieve the relatively narrow goal of economic growth. He encouraged governments to use a broader set of instruments – such as financial regulations and competition policy – to achieve a broader set of goals, including sustainable development, equity of income distribution and so on. Stiglitz's arguments are based on information asymmetry and the need for government to overcome market failures. He does not discuss how to deal with the issue of non-viable firms in developing and transitional economies, however, and the implications of non-viability for choices of transition path and policies.

[8] When reform started at the end of 1978 the government originally proposed raising the agricultural procurement prices, liberalising rural market fairs and reducing the size of production teams of twenty to thirty households to voluntarily formed production groups of three to five households, but explicitly prohibited the replacement of the production team system with an individual-household-based farming system. Nonetheless, a production team in a poor village in Fengyang county, Anhui province, secretly leased the collective-owned land to individual households in the team in the autumn of 1978 and harvested a bumper increase in outputs in 1979. Seeing the effects of the individual-household-based farming system, the government changed its policy and endorsed the system as a new direction for farming system reform (Lin, 1992). Initially the collectively owned land was leased to farm households for one to three years, then this period was extended to fifteen years in 1985, and further extended to thirty years in 1994. The farm household was obliged to deliver certain amounts of agricultural produce at the government-set prices to fulfil its quota obligation until the late 1990s.

[9] State-owned enterprise reform proceeded from the profit retention system in 1979, the contract responsibility system in 1986, and the modern corporation system from the 1990s to now. Each system was trialled in a small group of enterprises first before that system was extended nationwide (Lin, Cai and Li, 1994).

Weitzman and Xu, 1995). Then the government allowed collective township and village enterprises (TVEs),[10] private enterprises, joint ventures and state-owned enterprises to use the resources under their control to invest in labour-intensive industries that had been suppressed in the past. Meanwhile, the government required farmers and state-owned enterprises to fulfil their obligations to deliver certain quotas of products to the state at preset prices. The former reform improved the efficiency of resource allocation and the latter ensured the government's ability to continue subsidising the non-viable firms. Therefore, economic stability and dynamic growth were achieved simultaneously.

Finally, with the shrinking of the state-owned enterprises' share in the economy along with the dynamic growth path and the reduction in the need to subsidise state-owned enterprises, the government gradually eliminated price distortions and administrative allocation, and privatised the small and medium-sized enterprises – most of which were in the labour-intensive sectors and were consistent with China's comparative advantages (Lin, Cai and Li, 1994, 1996; Naughton, 1995; Nolan, 1995; Qian, 2003). Although there was no mass privatisation and the property rights of the collective township and village enterprises were ambiguous, market competition increased and economic performance was improved (Li, 1996; Lin, Cai and Li, 1998).

---

[10] The TVE was another institutional innovation by the peasants in China during the transition process. After the household responsibility system (HRS) reform, an individual-household-based farming system introduced as part of China's economic reforms (Lin, 1988), farmers obtained a substantial amount of residuals and saw profitable investment opportunities in the consumer products sector. Because of ideological reasons at the time, however, that form of private enterprise was prohibited, and the farmers used the collective TVE as an alternative in order to benefit from the profitable opportunity. The government initially put many restrictions on the operation of TVEs for fear of TVEs competing with state-owned enterprises for credits, resources, and markets. Only after the government had been convinced by the evidence that the TVE was good for increasing farmers' income and for solving the shortages in the urban markets did the government give the green light for the development of TVEs in rural China (Lin, Cai and Li, 1994).

The transitional strategy adopted by Vietnam has been similar to that employed in China. Through this cautious and gradual approach, China and Vietnam have been able to replace their traditional Soviet-type systems with a market system while maintaining remarkable records of growth and price stability.

Incidentally, since the 1970s Mauritius has also adopted a dual-track approach to opening up with its CAD-type strategy for an import substitution economy. It set up export-processing zones to encourage exports and maintained import restrictions to protect non-viable enterprises in domestic import-competing sectors. This reform strategy saw Mauritian GDP grow at 5.9 per cent per annum between 1973 and 1999 – an exceptional success story in Africa (Rodrik, 1999; Subramanian and Roy, 2003).

SIX

Development strategy, development and transition performances: empirical analysis

The previous chapters have discussed the effects of development strategy on institutional arrangements, economic growth, income distribution and transition performance in a country. From those discussions, I derive several testable hypotheses.

1 A country that adopts a CAD strategy will require various government interventions and distortions in its economy.
2 Over an extended period a country that adopts a CAD strategy will have poor growth performance.
3 Over an extended period a country that adopts a CAD strategy will have a volatile economy.
4 Over an extended period a country that adopts a CAD strategy will have less equitable income distribution.
5 In the transition to a market economy a country's overall economic growth will be improved if it creates conditions to facilitate the development of formerly repressed labour-intensive industries.

This chapter reports the results of empirical testing of the above hypotheses, some of which were conducted alongside my co-authors in previous studies.

6.1 Proxy for development strategy

In order to test the above hypotheses, a proxy for a country's development strategy is required. Lin and Liu (2004) propose a technology choice index (TCI) as a proxy for the development strategy implemented in a country. The definition of the TCI is as follows:

$$TCI_{i,t} = \frac{AVM_{i,t}/LM_{i,t}}{GDP_{i,t}/L_{i,t}} \tag{6.1}$$

where $AVM_{i,t}$ is the added value of manufacturing industries of country i at time t; $GDP_{i,t}$ is the total added value of country i at time t; $LM_{i,t}$ is the labour in the manufacturing industry; and $L_{i,t}$ is the total labour force. If a government adopts a CAD strategy to promote its capital-intensive industries, the TCI in this country is expected to be larger than it would otherwise be. This is because, if a country adopts a CAD strategy, in order to overcome the viability issue of the firms in the prioritised sectors of the manufacturing industries, the government might give the firms monopoly positions in the product markets – allowing them to charge higher output prices – and provide them with subsidised credits and inputs to lower their investment and operation costs. The above policy measures will result in a larger $AVM_{i,t}$ than otherwise. Meanwhile, investment in the prioritised manufacturing industry will be more capital-intensive and absorb less labour, *ceteris paribus*. The numerator in equation (6.1) will therefore be larger for a country that adopts a CAD strategy. As such, given the income level and other conditions, the magnitude of the TCI can be used as a proxy for the extent that a CAD strategy is pursued in a country.[1] The data for

---

[1] I have constructed another index (Lin, 2003) – based on the ratio of capital intensity in the manufacturing industry and the capital intensity in the whole economy – as a proxy for measuring the degree with which a CAD strategy is pursued. That proxy is correlated highly with the current proxy, and the results of empirical analyses based on that proxy are similar to the results reported in this section. The data for the capital used in a country's manufacturing industry are available for only a small number of countries, however. To enlarge the number of countries in the

calculating the TCI are taken from the World Bank's *World Development Indicators* (World Bank, 2002b) and the United Nations Industrial Development Organisation's *International Yearbook of Industrial Statistics* (UNIDO, 2002). The means and variations of the TCI for each of the 122 countries in the period 1963–99 are reported in appendix 2.

6.2 Development strategy and institutions

To assess the effects of development strategy on the government's distortions and interventions in the economy – as postulated in hypothesis (1) – I use several proxies for the institutions: (i) the 'black market premium' is used as an index of price distortion; (ii) the index of economic freedom (IEF) and the expropriation risk are used as indices of the government's intervention in property rights institutions; (iii) the number of procedures required for a start-up firm to obtain legal status and the 'executive de facto independence' are used as indices of enterprise autonomy; and (iv) the trade dependence ratio is used as an index for openness. The means and variations of each proxy for each country are reported in appendix 2.

6.2.1   *Development strategy and price distortion*
The black market premium of 105 countries is taken from the Global Development Network Growth Database produced by the Development Research Institute of New York University (NYU). The relationship between the TCI and the black market premium across four decades (1960–9, 1970–9, 1980–9 and 1990–9) is shown in figure 6.1.

The graphs in figure 6.1 show that the TCI and the black market premium had positive relationships throughout the four decades, which implies – as predicted by hypothesis (1) – that a higher

studies, I therefore use the proxy based on the added value of manufacturing industries as defined in equation (6.1) in this section.

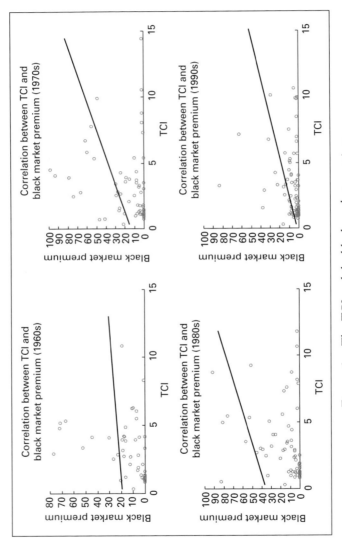

Figure 6.1 The TCI and the black market premium

degree of CAD strategy is associated with a larger black market premium.

6.2.2 Development strategy and government intervention in resource allocation

To measure government intervention in property rights institutions, I use the index of economic freedom and the expropriation risk. The observations constituting the IEF from ninety-one countries are taken from *Economic Freedom of the World* (Fraser Institute, 2007), and are available from 1970 onwards. This index ranges from zero to ten. The higher the value the higher the degree of economic freedom. The correlations between the TCI and the IEF averaged across a decade for each country are shown in figure 6.2.

There is a strong negative relationship between the TCI and the IEF in each of the panels of figure 6.2, which is consistent with the prediction that the more aggressively a government pursues a CAD strategy the more government invention is required, and the less economic freedom there is.

The expropriation risk of 102 countries is adopted from the *International Country Risk Guide* (Political Risk Services, 2007). The expropriation risk is the risk of outright confiscation and forced nationalisation of property. This variable ranges from zero to ten. A higher value means that a private enterprise has a lower probability of being expropriated. Figure 6.3 plots the relationship between the TCI and the expropriation risk. Both variables are calculated as the average values from 1982 until 1997.

As shown, there is a negative relationship between the TCI and expropriation risk, which is consistent with the expectation that the more aggressively a government adopts a CAD strategy the more likely it is that the government will confiscate or nationalise an enterprise.

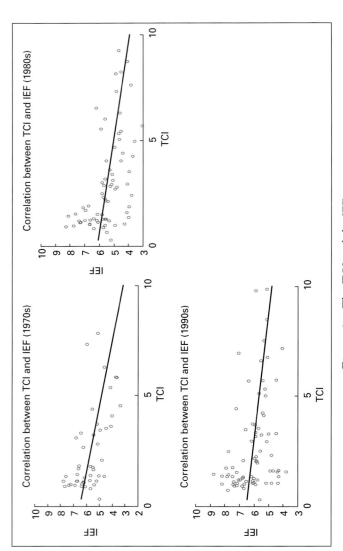

Figure 6.2 The TCI and the IEF

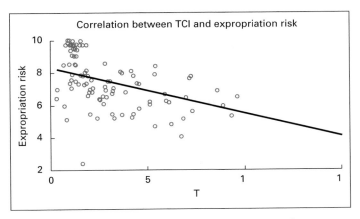

Figure 6.3 The TCI and expropriation risk

6.2.3 *Development strategy and enterprise autonomy*

To analyse the relationship between the government's development strategy and enterprise autonomy, the study uses two indices – including the number of procedures and the executive de facto independence used in Djankov *et al.* (2002) – to represent the extent of enterprise autonomy. There are sixty-nine countries in the samples.

The 'number of procedures' in figure 6.4 is the number of administrative procedures that a start-up firm has to comply with in order to obtain legal status – that is, to start operating as a legal entity. 'Executive de facto independence' is an index of 'operational (de facto) independence of the chief executive', descending from one to seven (1 = pure individual; 2 = intermediate category; 3 = slight to moderate limitations; 4 = intermediate category; 5 = substantial limitations; 6 = intermediate category; 7 = executive parity or subordination). Both indices are the average values for the years from 1965 until 1998.

The positive relationship between the TCI and the number of procedures and the negative relationship between the TCI and executive de facto independence shown in figure 6.4 indicate that a high degree of CAD strategy is associated with low enterprise autonomy, which confirms the prediction of hypothesis (1).

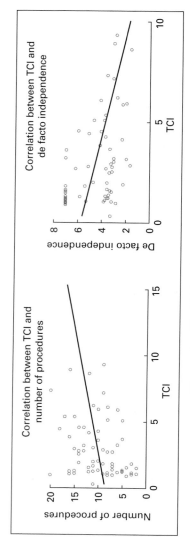

Figure 6.4 The TCI and enterprise autonomy

6.2.4 *Development strategy and openness*

The trade dependence ratio of 115 countries – taken from Dollar and Kraay (2003) – is used to reflect the openness of a country. The correlations between the TCI and openness averaged across the past four decades in each country are shown in figure 6.5.[2]

The TCI and openness have a negative relationship, which is consistent with the hypothesis that, if a developing country government adopts a CAD strategy, its economy will become more inward-oriented than otherwise. This is because the CAD strategy attempts to substitute the import of capital-intensive manufactured goods with domestic production, causing a reduction in imports. Exports will also be suppressed due to the inevitable transfer of resources away from the industries that have comparative advantage to the prioritised sectors determined by the CAD strategy. The more a country follows a CAD strategy, therefore, the less openness there will be in the country.

6.3 Development strategy and economic growth[3]

Hypothesis (2) predicts that, over an extended period, a country adopting a CAD strategy will have poor growth performance. The following econometric model is used to test the hypothesis:

$$GROWTH_{i,t} = C + \alpha TCI_{i,t} + \beta X + \xi \qquad (6.2)$$

where $GROWTH_{i,t}$ is the economic growth rate in a certain period in country i, and X is a vector that includes the initial per capita GDP to control the effect of the stage of development, the initial population size to control the effect of market size, an indicator of the rule of law to reflect institutional quality (which was constructed by Kaufmann, Kraay and Zoido-Lobatón, 2002) – the trade-dependent ratio to reflect openness, the distance from the equator and whether the country is

---

[2] The samples are eighty-six for the 1960s, ninety-seven for the 1970s, 107 for the 1980s and 114 for the 1990s.
[3] Sections 3, 4 and 6 draw on Lin and Liu (2004).

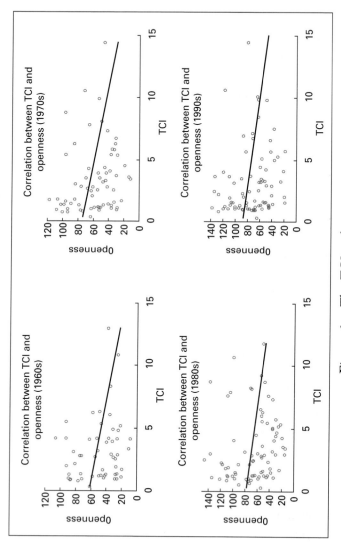

Figure 6.5 The TCI and openness

landlocked. The last two explanatory variables are included to capture the effects of geography. The instrumental variables for controlling the endogeneity of institutional quality are the fraction of the population that speaks English and the fraction that speaks a major European language (Hall and Jones, 1999), which are used to capture the long-run impacts of colonial origin on current institutional quality. Similarly, the fitted values of trade predicted by a gravity model are used as the instrument for openness. This approach was proposed by Frankel and Romer (1999) and revised by Dollar and Kraay (2003). In the regressions that use panel data, the instrument for openness is the single-period lagged value of itself. Table 6.1 summarises the definition of each variable and the data source.

Two approaches were used to test this hypothesis. In the first approach, the dependent variable is the average annual growth rate of per capita GDP for the period 1962 to 1999, and, in the second, the dependent variable is the average annual growth rate of per capita GDP for each decade of the 1960s, 1970s, 1980s and 1990s.

Table 6.2 reports the estimates from the first approach. Regression models 1.1 and 1.2 use an ordinary least squares (OLS) approach to obtain estimates. The explanatory variables in model 1.1 include only the proxy for the development strategy, LnTCI1, and the initial GDP per capita, LnGDP60, whereas model 1.2 includes other explanatory variables that capture institutional quality, openness, geographic location and market size. Model 1.3 has the same explanatory variables but the model uses the two-stage least squares (2SLS) approach in order to control the endogeneity of institutional quality and openness.

The results show that the TCI has the expected negative effect and is highly significant in all three regressions. This finding supports hypothesis (2), that the more aggressive the CAD strategy pursued by a country the worse the growth performance is in that country in the period 1962–99. The estimated coefficients of LnTCI1 have values ranging from −0.66 to −1.25. From the estimates, we can infer that a

TABLE 6.1 *Variable definition and data source*

Variable	Definition	Mean	Standard deviation	Sources
LnGDP60	Log of real GDP per capita in 1960	7.33	0.80	World Bank (2002b)
LnGDP80	Log of real GDP per capita in 1980	7.91	1.05	World Bank (2002b)
LnGDP	Log of real GDP per capita in 1960, 1970, 1980, 1990	7.73	1.02	World Bank (2002b)
LnTCI1	Log of the average technology choice index from 1963 to 1999	0.96	0.90	World Bank (2002b), UNIDO (2002)
LnTCI2	Log of the average TCI per decade in 1960s, 1970s, 1980s, 1990s	0.85	0.84	World Bank (2002b), UNIDO (2002)
LnTCI70	Log of the average TCI from 1970 to 1979; if not available, log of the average TCI from 1980 to 1985	0.91	0.92	World Bank (2002b), UNIDO (2002)
ΔTCI	Log of the average TCI from 1999 to 1990 minus LnTCI70	0.07	0.38	World Bank (2002b), UNIDO (2002)
RLo1	Rule of law in 2000–1	0.003	0.95	Kaufmann, Kraay and Zoido-Lobatón (2002)
LnOPEN1	Log of the average (exports + imports)/GDP from 1960 to 1999	−1.11	0.81	Dollar and Kraay (2003)
LnOPEN2	Log of the decadal average (exports + imports)/GDP in 1960s, 1970s, 1980s, 1990s	−1.30	0.84	Dollar and Kraay (2003)
LnPOP1	Log of the total mid-year population from 1960 to 1999	15.2	2.11	World Bank (2002b)

TABLE 6.1

Variable	Definition	Mean	Standard deviation	Sources
LnPOP2	Log of the total initial-year population in 1960s, 1970s, 1980s, 1990s	14.93	2.12	World Bank (2002b)
LANDLOCK	Dummy variable taking value of 1 if country is landlocked; 0 otherwise	0.18	0.39	Dollar and Kraay (2003)
LnDIST	Log (DISTEQ + 1), where DISTEQ is distance from equator, measured as absolute value of latitude of capital city	2.96	0.88	Dollar and Kraay (2003)
ENGFRAC	Fraction of population speaking English	0.07	0.24	Hall and Jones (1999), taken from Dollar and Kraay (2003)
EURFRAC	Fraction of population speaking a major European language	0.22	0.38	Hall and Jones (1999), taken from Dollar and Kraay (2003)
LnFRINST	Instrument variable for LnOPEN	−2.83	0.64	Dollar and Kraay (2003)
INST	Predicted value of RLo1 in the cross-section estimation (ENGFRAC and EURFRAC as the instruments)	0.003	0.34	

10 per cent increase from the mean in the TCI can result in approximately 0.1 of a percentage point reduction in the country's average annual growth rate of per capita GDP for the whole period 1962–99.

The regression results also show that the initial per capita income and the population size have the expected signs and significant effects on the growth rate. The rule of law, openness and the distance from the equator also have the expected signs. The rule of law is not

TABLE 6.2 *Development strategy and economic growth – 1*

	Model 1.1 (OLS)	Model 1.2 (OLS)	Model 1.3 (2SLS)
Constant	7.32*** (1.60)	4.66** (1.87)	3.26 (2.15)
LnTCI2	−1.25*** (0.20)	−0.66*** (0.18)	−0.92*** (0.19)
LnGDP60	−0.54*** (0.20)	−0.99*** (0.18)	−0.59*** (0.21)
RL01		0.58*** (0.21)	
INST			0.22 (0.41)
LnOPEN2		0.70*** (0.22)	
TRADE2			0.93** (0.43)
LnDIST		0.20 (0.16)	0.47*** (0.16)
LnPOP2		0.33*** (0.09)	0.22** (0.09)
LANDLOCK		0.07 (0.32)	0.46 (0.38)
Adjusted-R^2	0.36	0.56	0.44
Observations	85	83	83

Notes: The dependent variable is the yearly average of per capita GDP growth rate in 1962–99. ** indicates significance at the 5 per cent level; *** indicates significance at the 1 per cent level. Standard errors are reported in parentheses.

significant in the 2SLS regression, however, and the distance from the equator is not significant in the OLS regression. Whether the country is landlocked is insignificant in all three regressions.

Table 6.3 reports the results from the second approach, in which the dependent variable is the average annual growth rate of per capita GDP in each decade from 1960 to 1999. The regressions to fit the estimates are OLS for models 2.1 and 2.2, a one-way fixed effect for model 2.3, 2SLS for model 2.4 and 2SLS and a one-way fixed effect for model 2.5. In the fixed-effect models, time dummies are added to control the time effects, whereas the 2SLS models are used for controlling the endogeneity of institutional quality and openness.

As with the results in the first approach, the estimates for the TCI have the expected negative sign and are highly significant in all regressions. The finding is once again consistent with the prediction of hypothesis (2) that development strategy is a prime determinant of the long-run economic growth performance of a country. The results for the other explanatory variables are similar to those in table 6.2.

TABLE 6.3 *Development strategy and economic growth – 2*

	Model 2.1 (OLS)	Model 2.2 (OLS)	Model 2.3 (fixed effect)	Model 2.4 (2SLS)	Model 2.5 (2SLS, fixed effect)
Constant	7.15*** (1.61)	8.36*** (2.16)	3.83* (2.11)	−0.74 (2.56)	−2.70 (2.37)
LnTCI2	−1.10*** (0.21)	−0.69*** (0.20)	−0.40** (0.19)	−0.69*** (0.24)	−0.47** (0.22)
LnGDP	−0.54*** (0.18)	−1.39*** (0.23)	−0.86*** (0.23)	−0.17 (0.27)	0.17 (0.25)
RLoi		1.45*** (0.23)	1.12*** (0.22)		
INST				−0.38 (0.42)	−0.67* (0.38)
LnOPEN2		0.24 (0.23)	0.35 (0.22)	0.01 (0.29)	−0.06 (0.27)
TRADE2				0.27 (0.20)	0.17 (0.18)
LnDIST		−0.04 (0.18)	−0.10 (0.17)		
LnPOP2		0.32*** (0.10)	0.41*** (0.09)	0.22* (0.12)	0.27** (0.12)
LANDLOCK		−0.31 (0.39)	0.08 (0.36)	−0.23 (0.46)	0.02 (0.43)
Adjusted-R²	0.08	0.23	0.36	0.08	0.24
Observations	315	278	278	213	213

Notes: The dependent variable is the average growth rate of GDP per capita in the decades of the 1960s, 1970s, 1980s and 1990s. Models 2.3 and 2.5 include the time dummy. * indicates significance at the 10 per cent level; ** indicates significance at the 5 per cent level; *** indicates significance at the 1 per cent level. Standard errors are reported in parentheses.

6.4 Development strategy and economic volatility

Hypothesis (3) is about the effect of a CAD strategy on the volatility of the economic growth rate. If a country follows a CAD strategy, there could be a period of investment-led growth, but it will not be sustainable and is likely to cause economic crisis. Therefore, a country that follows a CAD strategy is likely to be more volatile than otherwise would be the case. In the empirical testing of this hypothesis, the volatility of a country's per capita GDP growth rate in the period 1962–99 is measured as follows:

$$
V_i = \left[(1/38) \sum_{t=1962}^{T=1999} \left(\frac{g_{it}}{\left(\sum_{t=1962}^{T=1999} g_{it} \right) \Big/ 38} - 1 \right)^2 \right]
\tag{6.3}
$$

where g_{it} is the growth rate of GDP per capita of ith country in year t.

In testing hypothesis (3), the dependent variable is the log of the above measurement of volatility, V_i, and the explanatory variables are the same as those used in testing hypothesis (2). The approaches to fitting the regression equation are also similar to those used previously. Table 6.4 reports the results from fitting the regression models. As expected, the estimates of the TCI are positive and highly significant in all three regressions. The results support hypothesis (3) and indicate that the more deeply a country follows a CAD strategy the more volatile the country's economic growth rate is. From the estimates, it can be inferred that a 10 per cent increase in the TCI could cause volatility to increase about 4 to 6 per cent.

The estimates for other explanatory variables show that the quality of institutions, the degree of openness, whether the country is landlocked and the population size all have negative effects on economic volatility. Except for the population size – which is a proxy for the size of the economy, and its coefficients are significant in the OLS and 2SLS models – the estimated coefficients for other variables

TABLE 6.4 *Development strategy and economic volatility*

	Model 3.1 (OLS)	Model 3.2 (OLS)	Model 3.3 (2SLS)
Constant	0.49 (1.06)	3.03** (1.44)	3.63** (1.56)
LnTCI1	0.64*** (0.13)	0.41*** (0.14)	0.56*** (0.14)
LnGDP60	−0.04 (0.13)	0.17 (0.14)	−0.07 (0.15)
RL01		−0.33** (0.16)	
INST			−0.20 (0.29)
LnOPEN1		−0.46*** (0.17)	
TRADE1			−0.53 (0.33)
LnDIST		−0.003 (0.11)	−0.15 (0.11)
LnPOP1		−0.26*** (0.06)	−0.18** (0.07)
LANDLOCK		−0.31 (0.24)	−0.53* (0.28)
Adjusted-R^2	0.29	0.47	0.37
Observations	103	93	93

Notes: The dependent variable is the log of the growth rate's volatility for GDP per capita from 1962 to 1999. * indicates significance at the 10 per cent level; ** indicates significance at the 5 per cent level; *** indicates significance at the 1 per cent level. Standard errors are reported in parentheses.

are significant in the OLS model and the 2SLS model. The estimates for the initial per capita income in 1960 and the distance from the equator are insignificant in all three regressions.

6.5 Development strategy and income distribution

In testing the effect of development strategy on income distribution, the following regression equation is used:

$$GINI_{i,t} = C + \alpha TCI_{i,t} + \beta X + \varepsilon \tag{6.4}$$

where $GINI_{i,t}$ is the index of inequality in country i at time t, TCI is a proxy for the development strategy and X is a vector of other explanatory variables.

GINI coefficients are taken from a revised version of the data set in Deininger and Squire (1996). The data set includes an estimation of GINI coefficients for many countries in the literature. Some are estimated according to the data on income; others are based

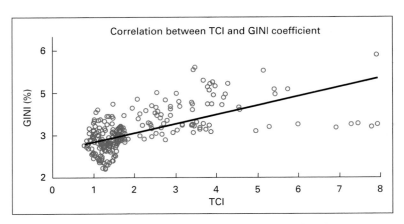

Figure 6.6 Development strategy and income distribution

on expenditure. The coverage differs between the different countries' GINI data. Deininger and Squire (1996) assess the quality of
GINI coefficient estimations; only those ranked as 'acceptable' are
used in the regression. The original estimates of GINI coefficients
based on income data are left unchanged, but those based on
consumption expenditure are adjusted by adding 6.6, which is
the average difference between the two estimation methods. For
details of the calculation of the TCI index and data sources, see
Lin and Liu (2003). Matching this GINI data with the TCI, I end up
with a panel of 261 samples from thirty-three countries. Figure 6.6
shows the relationship between the TCI and the GINI coefficient.

In order to test alternative hypotheses for the determination of
inequality, I have included the explanatory variables per capita
income, $GDPPC_{i,t}$, and its reciprocal, $GDPPC\_1_{i,t}$, which test the
Kuznets inverted-U hypothesis. If Kuznets' hypothesis holds, the
coefficients for these two variables should be significantly negative.[4]

Based on the data set of Deininger and Squire (1996), Li, Squire
and Zou (1998) conduct a robust empirical test, and the result shows
that the GINI coefficient for an individual country is relatively constant across different periods. Based on this conclusion, the GINI

[4] For this specification, refer to Deininger and Squire (1996).

coefficient in the initial year in the data set is introduced into the regression, denoted by 'IGINI'. In this way, the historical factors that could affect income distribution and those non-observable factors across countries can be excluded. In the data set, the year of IGINI differs from country to country. In spite of this difference, the higher the IGINI the higher the subsequent GINI coefficients are – regardless of the initial year. As a result, the coefficient of IGINI is expected to be positive.

Corruption could also affect income distribution. Two explanatory variables are included in the regression: the index for corruption, $CORR_{i,t}$, and the quality of officials, $BQ_{i,t}$. The data for these two variables are taken from Sachs and Warner (1999), and they differ from country to country but remain constant throughout the period studied. The larger the value is the less corruption there is and the higher the quality of officials is. The coefficients of these two variables are expected to be negative.

Foreign trade could also affect income distribution. It affects the relative prices of factors of production (Samuelson, 1978) and market opportunities for different sectors in the economy. Consequently, trade – through its effect on employment opportunities (Krugman and Obstfeld, 1997) – can affect income distribution. The regression therefore includes an index of economic openness, denoted by $OPEN_{i,t}$, which is the share of total import and export value in nominal GDP, as an explanatory variable. The data are taken from the Global Development Network Growth Database. Openness could, however, have different impacts on skilled and unskilled labour, on tradable and non-tradable sectors and in the short run and in the long run. Its sign is therefore uncertain.

Table 6.5 reports the results from five regression models. Model 4.1 includes all explanatory variables: TCI, IGINI, GDPPC, GDPPC_1, CORR, BQ and OPEN. As CORR, BQ and OPEN are endogenous, other models exclude these variables to control the endogeneity

TABLE 6.5 *The effect of development strategy on inequality*

	Model 4.1	Model 4.2	Model 4.3	Model 4.4	Model 4.5
Constant	6.46	8.18***	31.5***	8.09***	32.6***
	(4.72)	(2.40)	(1.75)	(3.16)	(0.97)
TCI	1.32***	1.35***	1.84***	1.35***	1.72***
	(0.33)	(0.31)	(0.48)	(0.32)	(0.46)
IGINI	0.73***	0.71***		0.71***	
	(0.08)	(0.07)		(0.07)	
GDPPC	−0.89		0.43	0.74	
	(11.3)		(12.6)	(10.8)	
GDPPC_1	0.40		1.91	3.21	
	(1.84)		(2.11)	(16.6)	
CORR	1.03*				
	(0.58)				
BQ	−0.84				
	(0.58)				
OPEN	0.12				
	(1.68)				
R^2	0.9040	0.8941	0.5495	0.8936	0.5780
Hausman statistics	3.32	1.19	23.91	1.99	7.98
Hausman P-value	0.19	0.28	0.00	0.37	0.00
Sample	261 observations from 33 countries				

Notes: Models 4.1, 4.2 and 4.4 are random-effect models, models 4.3 and 4.5 are fixed-effect models. * indicates significance at the 10 per cent level; *** indicates significance at the 1 per cent level. Null hypothesis of Hausman test: there is a random effect in countries and time. Standard errors are reported in parentheses.

problem. Because IGINI, CORR and BQ are time-invariant, the one-way effects model is applied in fitting the regression of models 4.1, 4.2 and 4.4. According to Hausman tests, the one-way random-effect model is used in the regressions of models 4.1, 4.2 and 4.4, and the two-way fixed-effect model is used in the regression of models 4.3 and 4.5.

The estimated coefficients of TCI are positive and significant at the 1 per cent level in all five regression models. These results strongly support the hypothesis that the more a country pursues a CAD strategy the more severe the income disparity will be in that country. This result holds whether the initial income distribution is equal or unequal.

The estimated coefficients of IGINI are also positive and significant at the 1 per cent level in models 4.1, 4.2 and 4.4. This result is consistent with the finding in Li, Squire and Zou (1998): that the initial income distribution will have a carry-over effect in the subsequent period's income distribution.

The estimated coefficients of GDPPC and GDPPC_1 in models 4.1, 4.3 and 4.4 are all insignificant and have an unexpected positive sign – except for GDPPC in model 4.1. Kuznets' inverted-U hypothesis of income distribution is therefore rejected.

The results in model 4.1 show that the coefficient for $CORR_{i,t}$ has an unexpected positive sign. One possible reason for this is that the effect of corruption on distribution is not reflected accurately in the surveys. The coefficient for bureaucracy quality, $BQ_{i,t}$, has an expected, but insignificant, negative sign. The coefficient for openness, OPEN, is positive, but not significant.

From the results above, it is clear that development strategy and initial income distribution are the two most important determinants of income distribution in a country. As I have argued, for a country in which the government follows a CAF strategy, income distribution will become more equal even if its initial income distribution is unequal. In effect, this is the 'growth with equity' phenomenon observed in Taiwan and other NIEs in East Asia (Fei, Ranis and Kuo, 1979).

6.6 Transition and economic performance

I have shown that the development of labour-intensive sectors – in which developing countries have a comparative advantage – is suppressed and many institutions are distorted if the government adopts a CAD strategy, resulting in poor resource allocation and inefficiency. The growth performance during the transition to a market economy depends, therefore, on the country's ability to create an enabling environment for the development of labour-intensive sectors and, at the same time, to find a way to solve the viability issue for firms inherited from the preceding development strategy so as to pave the way for eliminating the previous distortions and interventions. A CAD strategy is associated with a high TCI. If, after the reform/transition, a country is able successfully to develop labour-intensive sectors, resource allocation and growth performance will improve, and the TCI will decline. A successful transition from a CAD strategy is therefore expected to result in a negative change in the TCI. The larger the negative change the higher the expected growth rate. For the purposes of testing hypothesis (5), therefore, a variable, ΔTCI, is created to measure the difference between the log of the average TCI in the period 1990–9 and the log of the average TCI in the period 1970–9 – as the transition in socialist countries and the reforms in other developing countries started in the 1980s.

The dependent variable in the regressions is the log of the average annual growth rate of GDP per capita in the period 1980–99. In addition to ΔTCI, the explanatory variables include the log of average TCI in the 1970s, initial per capita GDP in 1980 and other explanatory variables – representing institutional quality, openness and population size – that are similar to those used in testing hypothesis (1).

Two approaches are used to test the hypothesis. The first includes observations from all countries in the data set, while the second includes only the developing countries defined in the Global Development Network Growth Database. Both approaches try three regressions – two by OLS and one by 2SLS – to control the endogeneity problem of institutional quality and openness. Table 6.6 reports the results from the regressions.

As expected, the sign of ΔTCI is negative and the estimates are significantly different from zero in all six regressions. The results support the hypothesis that the larger the reduction in the TCI from the level in the 1970s to the level in the 1990s the larger the positive effect on the average per capita GDP growth rate in the period

TABLE 6.6 Development strategy and the performance of economic reform/transition

	Model 5.1 (OLS)	Model 5.2 (OLS)	Model 5.3 (2SLS)	Model 5.4 (OLS)	Model 5.5 (OLS)	Model 5.6 (2SLS)
Constant	2.53 (3.17)	3.79 (3.63)	-2.94 (3.97)	4.28 (4.24)	-4.50 (5.01)	-9.03 (6.43)
ΔTCI	-1.25** (0.55)	-0.91** (0.45)	-1.12** (0.51)	-1.16* (0.66)	-1.02* (0.52)	-1.30** (0.60)
LnTCI$_{70}$	-0.84** (0.41)	-0.38 (0.34)	-0.52 (0.38)	-0.61 (0.48)	-0.26 (0.38)	-0.31 (0.45)
LnGDP$_{80}$	-0.04 (0.35)	-1.32*** (0.37)	-0.31 (0.38)	-0.34 (0.50)	-0.78* (0.45)	-0.12 (0.57)
RL$_{01}$		1.31*** (0.37)			1.78*** (0.47)	0.96 (1.18)
INST		0.71* (0.36)	0.44 (0.60)		0.54 (0.49)	
LnOPEN$_1$						
TRADE$_1$			1.50** (0.70)			2.23* (1.26)
LnDIST		0.16 (0.28)	0.57* (0.29)		-0.06 (0.33)	0.34 (0.36)
LnPOP$_1$		0.52*** (0.17)	0.44*** (0.16)		0.79*** (0.19)	0.78** (0.29)
LANDLOCK		-0.87 (0.57)	-0.06 (0.68)		-0.55 (0.73)	0.54 (1.15)
Adjusted-R^2	0.13	0.43	0.27	0.03	0.45	0.24
Observations	76	72	72	50	49	49

Notes: The dependent variable is the average growth rate of GDP per capita from 1980 to 1999. The data samples in the regression of models 6.4–6.6 include only the developing countries defined in the Global Development Network Growth Database. * indicates significance at the 10 per cent level; ** indicates significance at the 5 per cent level; *** indicates significance at the 1 per cent level. Standard errors are reported in parentheses.

1980–99. For a country that adopts a CAD strategy, therefore, growth performance will be improved if the government manages well the transition from a CAD to a CAF strategy. From the estimates, we can infer that a 10 per cent reduction in the TCI level in the 1990s to the level of the 1970s could cause a 0.1–0.13 percentage point increase in the average annual growth rate of per capita GDP in the period 1980–99.

The other explanatory variables all have the expected signs; except for the population size, which is positive and highly significant in all six regressions, however, the other variables are either insignificant or significant in some regressions but not in others.

In a nutshell, as predicted by hypothesis (5), the entry of small and medium-sized firms into the repressed sectors under a CAD strategy is essential for the economy to achieve dynamic growth during the transition process.

6.7 Concluding remarks

The above empirical evidence strongly suggests that it is the development strategy that is the fundamental determinant of a country's institutional quality, economic performance and income distribution. If the government in a developing country adopts a CAD strategy, it will suppress factor prices and prompt various institutional distortions to protect and subsidise the non-viable firms in the prioritised industries, which will in turn repress incentives and worsen resource allocation, resulting in poor growth performance and causing the growth rate to be volatile. A CAD strategy will lead also to the unequal distribution of income in the economy. During economic reform and transition, a country's economic performance depends on its government's ability to create an environment that facilitates the growth of labour-intensive industries, which have been suppressed in the past due to the government's pursuit of a CAD strategy.

SEVEN

Why are east Asian economies so special? Are there any general lessons to be learnt from east Asian development and transition experiences?

East Asian economies seem to be rather special in terms of their development and transition performance since the Second World War. Development 'miracles' occurred in the NIEs in east Asia and transitional miracles in China and Vietnam. If, as I have argued, social thought is the deepest and most fundamental determinant of government policy and social and economic institutions in a country – in turn determining a country's economic performance – why is it that, despite the prevailing social thinking about develop-ment in the 1950s and 1960s and about transition in the 1980s and 1990s, the east Asian governments behaved so differently and achieved such miraculous economic success? My analysis is incom-plete without an answer to this question.

As discussed, China, Vietnam and other east Asian economies adopted a dual-track, gradualist approach in their transition from centrally planned economies to market economies, which violated the basic tenets of the Washington Consensus and the shock therapy treatment. In effect, for its transition from a wartime economy after the Second World War, Japan also adopted a gradual approach, whereas Germany adopted a big-bang approach (Teranishi, 1994). In terms of the development policies in South

Korea and Taiwan, both governments initially adopted a policy mix – including financial repression, overvalued exchange rates, deficit budgets and neglect of the agricultural sector – to support the development of labour-intensive primary manufacturing industries in order to reduce the need for imports of manufactured household products: a policy referred to as 'primary import substitution'. The policy package was typical in countries that adopted a CAD strategy. What differentiated South Korea and Taiwan from other developing countries were two factors, as discussed by Ranis and Mahmood (1992). First, after they had succeeded in primary import substitution, they relied on their abundant labour resources and turned to primary export substitution: they changed their export mix from primarily land-intensive agricultural products to labour-intensive manufactured products instead of jumping to 'secondary import substitution' – that is, attempting to develop big, heavy industries to reduce the need for imports of capital-intensive machinery and equipment, which is what many other developing countries did. They did not move to the 'secondary import-cum-export substitution' phase until labour shortages occurred, real wages increased and the comparative advantages in labour-intensive industries were lost in the international markets. Second, the repression in the financial sector and the overvaluation of the exchange rate were rather mild. The real interest rate was kept positive at all times and the difference between the exchange rate on the black market and the official market was small. Therefore, the government's policy mix was close to what I have advocated: providing information and overcoming the issues of coordination and externality in the process of industrial upgrading by effectively becoming a facilitating state. The industrial upgrading in Taiwan and South Korea has basically followed their comparative advantages in each stage of their economic development. Similarly, in post-war Japan, the main industries upgraded from labour-intensive to capital-intensive industries in sequence – textiles, simple machine tools, steel, shipbuilding, electronics, automobiles and computers – according to changes in comparative advantages (Ito, 1998; Shinohara, 1982). Singapore and Hong Kong also followed a similar pattern in their economic development (World Bank, 1993).

It was not the intentional choice of the government in Japan and other east Asia economies to follow a CAF strategy in pursuit of economic development. Under the influence of prevailing social thought in the 1950s and 1960s, governments in east Asia also had a strong desire for the development of advanced capital-intensive industries – just like governments in other developing countries at that time. Their economies were relatively small in population size and their natural resource endowments were extremely poor. This greatly constrained their ability to mobilise enough resources to subsidise the non-viable enterprises in the capital-intensive industries in the early stage of their development (Lin, Cai and Li, 1996; Ranis and Mahmood, 1992).

For example, in the early 1950s Taiwan was influenced by the fashionable post-war development thinking and tried to protect and subsidise the development of heavy industries by using quantitative restrictions, tariff barriers and subsidised credits via the strict regulation of banks and other financial intermediaries. The attempt caused severe budget deficits and high inflation, however. The Taiwanese government had to give up the attempt; it devalued its currency, liberalised trade and raised the real interest rate to encourage savings and contain inflation (Tsiang, 1984). Without preferential protection and subsidisation, industrial upgrading in Taiwan followed closely the changes in its comparative advantages.

Similarly, the South Korean government, under the leadership of President Park Chung Hee, adopted an ambitious heavy and chemical industry drive in 1973. Nevertheless, it was adopted only after rapid economic growth had been achieved by developing and exporting labour-intensive textiles, plywood, wigs and other light industrial products for more than a decade since the early 1960s. Therefore, the drive reflected to some extent a necessity arising from the demand for industrial upgrading. It was too ambitious, however, causing the inflation rate, measured by the consumer price index, to jump from 3.1 per cent in 1972 to 24.3 per cent in 1973 and 25.3 per cent in 1974, and to remain at double-digit rates throughout the rest of the 1970s. By late 1978 and early 1979 President Park was increasingly concerned with stabilisation and social welfare, and, after his assassination in October 1979, the South Korean government – like the Taiwanese government in the 1950s – reined back its support to heavy and chemical industries (Stern *et al.*, 1995).[1]

A CAD strategy is very inefficient. How long such a strategy can be maintained depends on the level of resources the government can mobilise to subsidise the non-viable enterprises and to support its investment in the prioritised industries. Resource mobilisation is

---

[1] Compared with most other developing countries, South Korea's industrial upgrading has followed quite closely its comparative advantage at each stage of its development, which can be inferred from the fact that South Korean products remained competitive in international markets once the government had helped the enterprises with the initial supports and protection to build up the production capacities. The enterprises in these industries are therefore clearly viable. Compared with Taiwan, however, South Korea's development strategy after the 1970s was more ambitious, and the South Korean government was required to give protection for longer and more subsidies to its enterprises than Taiwan did. As the model by Krugman (1987) suggests, the heavy and chemical drive in the 1970s changed the human capital endowment in South Korea through the effect of learning by doing, enabling South Korean enterprises to jump from OEM (original equipment manufacture) directly to OBM (original brand manufacture), while Taiwanese enterprises in general followed step by step from OEM to ODM (original design manufacture) and finally to OBM (Lee, 2007). South Korea today is quite competitive in capital-intensive industries, such as steel, shipbuilding, automobiles and electronics, and these industries in general are heavier than in Taiwan. Taiwan's economic performance, however – measured in terms of the economic growth rate, per capita income levels and macro-stability – has been better than South Korea's. Taiwan weathered the east Asian financial crisis in the late 1990s without much harm, while the South Korean economy encountered a severe meltdown and was forced to accept a conditional IMF rescue. In the past few years the South Korean economy has outperformed the Taiwanese economy, though Taiwan's relatively poor performance is probably the result of its government's policies to obstruct the further integration of the Taiwanese economy with the economy of mainland China. In contrast, the South Korean government has been supportive of integration between its economy and the Chinese economy.

constrained by the natural resource endowment and population size. Contrasting with the case of the 'resource curse' in many parts of the developing world (Diamond, 1997; Pomeranz, 2000; Sachs and Warner, 1997, 2001), the east Asian economies were lucky in the sense that their governments needed to be pragmatic in their policies and unintentionally followed a CAF strategy – even though their governments had strong motivations for nation building and were influenced by the same prevailing social thought.[2]

In fact, pragmatism has long been the guiding principle of east Asia's traditional culture. China's Confucianism – which has a strong impact in east Asia – is pragmatic in nature. The core of Confucianism is 'zhongyong', the golden mean, which advises people to maintain balance, avoid extremes and achieve harmony with the outside, changing world. The political philosophy and policy principles promoted by the communist leadership of Mao Zedong, Deng Xiaoping, Jiang Zemin and Hu Jingtao are, respectively, 'shishiqiushi' (finding truth from the facts), 'jiefangsixiang' (freeing one's mind from dogmatism), 'yushijujin' (adapting to the changing environment) and 'hexie' (harmony) – all reflective of the traditional Chinese culture of zhongyong.

When Deng Xiaoping started his reforms in 1979, in addition to his philosophy of freeing one's mind from the dogmatism of the left and the right, the adoption of a gradual, piecemeal approach could also have reflected the political constraints he faced. Deng was one of the first generation of political leaders, who had started the socialist revolution, and he was involved in introducing a planned economy to China. In an Asian society, the power of a leader is based mainly on the personal prestige that a leader receives from the

---

[2] An example is China's Great Leap Forward in 1958–60, which aimed to use China's vast population to transform the country rapidly from a primarily agrarian economy dominated by peasant farmers to a modern, industrialised society. The result was a great famine in 1959–61, which led directly to some 30 million deaths (Lin, 1990; Lin and Yang, 2000).

people, rather than on the office he or she holds,[3] and it is hard for a leader to renounce policies that he or she pursued in the past for fear of losing his/her prestige in people's minds.[4] Therefore, when Deng replaced Mao as China's supreme leader after the death of Mao in 1976, it was natural for Deng not to denounce and discard the old system totally but to carry out piecemeal, tinkering, Pareto-improving changes to the old system. Similarly, the reforms in Vietnam and other east Asian economies were initiated by the first-generation revolutionaries who had originally brought socialism and planned economies to their countries.

Ideas and social thoughts can be shaped by people's experiences. My first visit to India was in 1988, to attend the inauguration conference of the Indira Ghandi Institute of Development Research in Mumbai. I visited four other cities – Kolkata, Madurai, Ahmadabad and New Delhi – and met Indian economists. I found that many Indian economists were suspicious of the success of China's reforms, and they repeatedly questioned the reliability of China's statistical data. I had the impression that they were quite pessimistic about the possibility of carrying out fundamental change and breaking the Indian growth rate of about 3 per cent per annum, which they referred as the 'Hindu rate of growth'. After 1988 I visited India again every three or four years, and, on each trip, I found that Indian economists' perceptions of China's reforms were becoming increasingly favourable, and India's own reforms gained momentum. The Indian economy has been growing at a rate of about 6–8 per cent for the past two decades. The unbreakable 'Hindu equilibrium' – a term used to describe the age-old combination of economic stagnation and cul-

---

[3] In his final years, Deng's only formal title was as honorary chairman of China's Bridge Society. He was, however, the de facto supreme leader until his death.

[4] In China, a leader's prestige is accumulated through the merits of his/her contributions to the people and the nation during his/her career, and people's trust of his/her wisdom to provide good guidance for the nation's future. If a political leader openly admits that he/she had made a mistake in a major area of policy in the past, people may lose their confidence in his/her wisdom, and his/her prestige will be hurt.

tural stability by Deepak Lal (2005) – has started to shatter. I do not know how large the impact of China's success has been on India's reform. I do, however, see clearly that most economists' thinking about the role of government and the market have changed in the past two decades, and a new, pro-market social thought has emerged and become dominant in India.

Before I answer the question of whether east Asia's success – especially its transitional experience – has general implications for other developing and transitional economies, I need to provide an analysis of the failure of gradual reforms in Poland, Hungary and the former Soviet Union in the 1980s before their adoption of shock therapy. These countries also tried to reform their planning systems by giving state-owned enterprises more autonomy. Their partial reforms did not, however, have the positive results of those in China and Vietnam. A number of explanations are in order. First, unlike in China and Vietnam – where state-owned enterprises, after fulfilling their plan obligations, were allowed to sell their extra output at market prices – the enterprises in eastern Europe and the former Soviet Union were not allowed to set their prices (Sachs, 1993: 28). This price rigidity meant that excess demand and chronic shortages remained, and the state producers did not have the incentives to allocate their products to more efficient users, who were able to pay higher prices for their products. Second, market entry by non-state enterprises were subject to severe restrictions (Kornai, 1986). Production remained monopolised and international trade was centrally regulated (Sachs and Lipton, 1990). Resource allocations were not improved, and therefore the existing state-owned enterprises never faced real competitive pressure from domestic or international sources and lacked the incentives to improve productivity. Third, in the traditional Soviet-type system, to prevent managerial discretion under the distorted macro-policy environment, state-owned enterprises were not allowed to set their workers' wage level. In the Chinese case, after profit-sharing arrangements had been introduced to the state-owned enterprises, wages were still controlled by the state. A worker's wage could increase only if the enterprise's profits exceeded a preset level. In Poland, Hungary and the former Soviet Union, however, partial reforms gave the enterprises the autonomy to set their workers' wages. The weakening of state control on wages gave managers and workers an opportunity to increase their incomes at the expense of the state by absorbing whatever income flow and whatever assets they could obtain from state-owned enterprises. The state's revenues were thus greatly curtailed.[5] Fourth, wage inflation caused the shortage to become even more acute. Governments in Poland and in the former Soviet Union then tried to play a populist game: they increased the imports of consumer goods and forced a heavy burden of foreign debt on their countries (Aslund, 1991). Because of this, instead of bringing continuous growth and a gradual transition to a market economy – as in China and Vietnam – the partial reforms led Poland and the former Soviet Union to the brink of bankruptcy and hyperinflation.

The transition from a CAD-type economy to a market economy in socialist and developing countries proved difficult. A transitional economy's institutions will inevitably be underdeveloped and in poor shape due to the government's heavy interventions and there will be severe distortions in prices and production structures. Shock therapy – which characterises a macro-first approach to building up the requisite market institutions – cannot deliver a 'rapid jump' to a prosperous market economy. The experiences in China and other east Asian economies show that deep and extensive reforms are not required for dynamic growth at the onset of a transition (Rodrik, 2003). As such, the crucial issue in transition is to have a strategy of sequencing reforms that identifies the most pressing bottlenecks and

---

[5] China and Vietnam also encountered this problem to some extent. In spite of the increase in productivity, the profitability of the state-owned enterprises declined. As a result, the government's fiscal revenue from the state-owned enterprises was reduced substantially (McKinnon, 1995).

concentrates resources on the relaxation of binding constraints, removing the suppression of incentives and inspiring people to improve performance to achieve a better life by their own efforts (McKinnon, 1993; Rawski, 1995).

The IMF/World Bank's macro-first reform approach might be appropriate for an economy in which market institutions are more or less intact and the structural imbalance is small. To use the famous analogy in a somewhat different version, 'When the chasm is narrow, it's all right to jump over it.' The stabilisation programme can then achieve its goal immediately and the economy can soon operate in a normal market environment. In a country that has pursued a CAD strategy for a long time with severe distortions and a large number of non-viable enterprises, the chasm will be too wide and too deep. A jump without careful preparation will result in a disastrous fall. In such a situation, it is desirable to fill and narrow the chasm before making the jump. The east Asian experience suggests that, with a small change that provides the right incentives for people, it is possible to unleash dynamic growth on a weak institutional base, leading to an eventual transition to a fully fledged, well-functioning market economy. For a developing country that follows a CAD strategy, there are bound to be distortions in the incentive system, which suppress individual efforts in production, and there will inevitably be industries that are consistent with the economy's comparative advantages but that are repressed. The useful lessons from the gradual, dual-track, micro-first approach to transition in east Asia can be summarised as follows.

- The government can take measures to improve individual incentives by granting partial managerial autonomy and profit sharing to farms and state-owned enterprises in order to improve incentives and allow the economy to move closer to the production frontier, which will induce a new stream of output growth. In choosing the measures, the government should pay special attention to spontaneous reform experiments arising from private and local initiatives. Fundamentally, it is the entrepreneurs among peasants, workers and local officials who best understand the institutional constraints they face, and it is to them that the new profitable opportunities appear.

- The government can introduce a dual-track price and allocation system to replace the old single-track plan. It can remove market entry restrictions to allow resources to be allocated increasingly by the non-state sector to the previously suppressed, more productive industries, while maintaining the quota obligations of state-owned enterprises and farms in order to secure adequate resources to subsidise the existing non-viable enterprises.[6]
- When the products in a sector are allocated largely by the market track, it is time for the government to introduce full market liberalisation in the sector.
- The government should introduce on an ongoing basis the necessary regulations and laws to strengthen market institutions during the above process.

The above principles or experiences of other countries should not be applied in a dogmatic way. One example is China's reform in 1979 of its household responsibility system, which leased collectively owned land to farm households for fifteen years. Like many reforms in China, it was initiated by farmers, sanctioned by the government and introduced nationwide only after its performance had been demonstrated. This reform resulted in a dramatic increase in agricultural productivity and output growth (Lin, 1992). The government of the former Soviet Union under Mikhail Gorbachev adopted similar reforms of its state farms with fifty-year leases. In theory, the Soviet reform seemed to be better than the Chinese reform, because of its longer and more secure tenure arrangement; the Soviet government

---

[6] Prices here include foreign exchange rates, wage rates, interest rates and the prices of all products and services.

had a hard time finding farmers willing to accept this arrangement, however. With hindsight, the failure of the Soviet Union's reforms may have been because its state farms were highly mechanised, depended heavily on purchased inputs – such as chemical fertilisers and fuel – in the production process and were far away from markets. As such, a small individual household farm was not viable. The opposite was true in China. In a gradual, piecemeal reform, therefore, the government should not have a predetermined, grand blueprint. Instead, it should follow a diagnostic approach, finding out the most crucial binding constraints on incentives and resource allocation and introducing reform measures that are effective but that can be regarded as 'halfway measures' by market fundamentalists – as argued recently by Hausmann, Rodrik and Velasco (2006). In the process, the government should encourage and pay attention to local and private initiatives in institutional innovations – as demonstrated convincingly by the experiences in China and the stories of Easterly (2006).[7] In this regard, political wisdom derived from Chinese culture – *shishiqiushi* (finding truth from the facts), *jiefangsixiang* (freeing one's mind from dogmatism) and *yushijujin* (adapting to the changing environment) – could be relevant to reform-minded governments in other developing and transitional countries.

---

[7] In effect, in addition to the individual-household-based farming system and the township and village enterprises, most other reforms in China were tried or experimented first with the initiatives of local entrepreneurs or governments, and were extended nationwide only after the initiatives' success had been demonstrated (Naughton, 1995).

EIGHT

Towards a right development and transition strategy

Freedom of the will . . . means nothing but the capacity to make decisions with knowledge of the subject.

Friedrich Engels (1877)

So far, what I have argued is as follows.

- Continuous technological upgrading is the most important driving
  force for a country's long-term dynamic growth in modern times. By
  tapping into the advantage of backwardness, a developing country
  has the opportunity to upgrade technology rapidly and to catch up
  and converge with developed countries' per capita income levels.
- Ideas are the most vital determinants of whether a developing
  country will be able to achieve long-term dynamic growth. With
  the guidance of right ideas, a developing country will be able to
  exploit the advantage of backwardness, achieve dynamic growth
  and converge with developed countries. Historical evidence
  shows, however, that the ideas reflected in the prevailing social
  thought about how a developing country should develop its
  economy are not correct because the ideas mistakenly took the
  result of development – that is, possessing advanced industries in
  a country – as the *cause* of development in a country.

- The government is the most important institution in a developing country. The policies pursued by the government will shape the quality of other institutions and the incentive structure in the economy. Political leaders run the government. Therefore, it is necessary to understand their motivations and behaviour in order to understand the country's policies. Political leaders' motivations are not necessarily selfish – as Alfred Marshall indicated – especially for those leaders who fight for their nation's independence and prosperity. Political leaders' behaviour and policy choices are shaped by the prevailing social thinking of their times, as well as domestic and economic constraints. With the best of intentions, political leaders can adopt incorrect policies and bring about a failure of government in the country's development.

- A country's endowments are the most important binding constraint on its choice of technology and industry. Endowments can be accumulated and altered through time. At any given time, they determine the total budget of the country, and the endowment structure – that is, the relative abundance of human and physical capital, labour and natural resources – determines the relative prices of capital, labour and natural resources, which in turn determine endogenously the most competitive technologies and industries in the country at that time.

- Comparative advantage is the most important guiding principle not just for trade but also for economic development in a developing country. A developing country that relies on its comparative advantage to guide its choice of industry and technology will be most competitive in domestic and international markets, producing the largest possible economic surplus, accumulating the most capital possible and upgrading its endowment structure as well as its technology and industry in the fastest possible way. As such, the country will attain the fastest rate of convergence with developed countries. On the other hand, if a developing country attempts to violate its comparative advantage in its choice of industry and technology, the economy will not be competitive in domestic and international markets. Not only will the country be unable to converge with developed countries, it could encounter stagnation and various crises.

- Viability is the most important concept in understanding the cause of various institutional distortions in developing countries. An enterprise will be viable in a competitive market only if its technology and industrial choices are consistent with its comparative advantage, determined by the economy's endowment structure. Due to the influence of inappropriate ideas in the prevailing social thought, however, most developing country governments attempt to develop excessively capital-intensive industries, making the enterprises in the priority industries non-viable. Governments are consequently obliged to provide the non-viable enterprises with protection and subsidies through various distortions. The institutional distortions are therefore endogenous to the viability constraints of the enterprises.

- Pragmatism is the most important policy guidance for economic transition. In developing countries' economic reforms and socialist countries' transitions to a market economy, policy recommendations based on the Washington Consensus are not adequate because they are based on assumptions that all enterprises in an economy are viable and the existing distortions are exogenous. A gradual, piecemeal approach to reform and transition – designed diagnostically and pragmatically in line with the actual situation 'on the ground' – could enable a country to achieve stability and dynamic growth simultaneously and allow it to complete its transition to a market economy.

- Spontaneous innovations from private and local initiatives are the most important sources of Pareto-improvement policy measures for reforming an economy with many second best or even nth best distortions. Most distortions are endogenous due to certain real-world constraints. It is easy to understand the costs and consequences of these distortions. It is infeasible in most cases to jump to the first best institutional arrangements without removing the constraints that led the economy to have those distortions in the first place, however, and it is also hard for outsiders to understand what those constraints are and how to carry out a gradual, piecemeal, Pareto-improvement reform programme with many distortions. Entrepreneurs among farmers, workers and local officials can best understand the constraints they face, and the profitable opportunities that appear to them. Therefore, in carrying out a pragmatic, Pareto-improvement, gradual reform policy, the government should encourage private and local initiatives, pay special attention to those successful, spontaneous innovations, summing up the lessons of those innovations, and introduce those innovations that enhance the incentives and increase the allocation of resources to repressed, comparative-advantage-consistent sectors as national reform policies.

Under their governments' leadership, the east Asian economies have been able to exploit the opportunities provided by the advantage of backwardness, and they have achieved convergence with developed countries. China and Vietnam have been successful in achieving dynamic growth in their transition to market economies. These successes reflect the importance of their governments' policy choices because of their inability to follow the dominant social thinking due to their resource constraints. With their development policies closely following their comparative advantages and their transition policies designed pragmatically – and with the high social capacity inherited from their long-established civilizations – the east Asian economies have created one miracle after another in terms of economic development and transition since the end of the Second World War.

The success of the east Asian economies has involved an element of luck. Resource constraints and a long-established civilisation are not necessary or sufficient conditions for economic success, however – as demonstrated by the success of Botswana and Mauritius in Africa and Chile in South America. I therefore share Lewis's (1955: 418) optimism: '[A]ll nations have opportunities which they may grasp if only they can summon up the courage and the will.' From so many stories of success and failure in economic development and transition in modern times, again I agree with Lewis's judgement that 'it is possible for a nation to take a new turn if it is fortunate to have the right leadership at the right time'. Political leaders certainly worry about their security of tenure in office and their own place in the nation's history. The best way to ensure security of tenure and historical standing – regardless of the political system – is to bring prosperity to the nation. All political leaders in developing countries can therefore be safely said to have the internal motivation to do good for their country. The success or failure of economic development and transition in a developing country need not be a matter of destiny, if its political leader knows what the right policies for the nation are.

I hope that this book will make a small contribution to the knowledge that helps developing and transitional countries jump from the kingdom of necessity to the kingdom of freedom in their pursuit of economic development and transition to a developed, wealthy market economy.

Development strategy and economic institutions in developing countries

A1.1 Introduction

As discussed in the lectures, after the Second World War, governments in developing countries – socialist and non-socialist – instituted a complicated set of regulations and distortions that suppressed the functions of markets, such as financial depression, trade restriction, the rationing of capital and foreign exchange, the licensing of investments, administrative monopoly and state ownership. It has now been recognised that, no matter what the motivation might be, these policies often led to poor economic performance, low living standards and even frequent crises in developing countries. Despite the many competing hypotheses about the causes and effects of these regulations and distortions, none has revealed, convincingly, the internal logic among the various policies in the complicated set of regulations and distortions.

This appendix has been prepared with the help of Pengfei Zhang, Binkai Chen and Zhaoyang Xu, all members of the CCER Development Workshop. Seminar participants at NYU provided helpful comments and suggestions. Much of Zhang's work was completed at the Center for International Development, Harvard University and the National Bureau of Economic Research. Zhang would like to thank Martin Feldstein, Ricardo Hausman and Dani Rodrik, as well as these two organisations, for their kind hospitality.

The classical theory for government regulations (Pigou, 1938) has been called the 'helping hand' view. Seeing the adverse effects of government regulations and distortions in developing countries, economists have proposed an alternative 'grabbing hand' view (Acemoglu, 2007b; Grossman and Helpman, 1994; Shleifer and Vishny, 1994; Sokoloff and Engerman, 2000). These authors propose that government interventions were pursued for the benefit of politicians and bureaucrats – for example, favouring friendly firms and other political constituencies so as to obtain benefits such as campaign contributions and votes[1] or benefiting selected groups within a country that had unusually strong political influence.

While government regulations and distortions in developing countries could theoretically arise from rent extraction by the government or political elites, understanding the complexity of such policies remains an unsolved question in the literature. In developing countries, the institutional arrangements shaped by government intervention are quite complicated. What are the governments' incentives to institute such a complicated system, which increases the costs of expropriations and political control and diminishes the gains to be had by grabbing? Corruption induced by special interest groups might not be a good explanation either, because the groups that benefit from certain regulations are often taxed or suppressed along with the protections and/or subsidies. In fact, many interventions do not even have obvious beneficiary groups (Lin *et al.*, 2007).

Beyond the arguments from the helping and grabbing-hand categories, some recent theoretical work suggests that government regulations and distortions in developing countries might be designed to alleviate the problems of tax collection. Gordon and Li (2005a, 2005b) argue that tax enforcement depends heavily on the availability of information outside a firm and on the scale of its economic

---

[1] A study prepared by Djankov *et al.* (2002) provides an empirical test of the grabbing hand theories, and suggests that a barrier for business entry might arise from the corruption of bureaucrats.

activities. Such information comes largely from the firm's recorded transactions through the financial sector. Most production activities in a developing country are in the informal economy and rely on cash transactions – and are virtually impossible to monitor and tax. Gordon and Li argue that tariff protection is used to compensate firms in the formal sectors that face high effective tax rates, and lending control is used to redirect credit to heavily taxed sectors. They also argue that inflation is used as a tax on firms that rely on cash to avoid tax, and red tape and fees are used to impose non-tax costs on businesses that in practice pay little or no taxes. Esfahani (2000) proposes that, as administrative weakness becomes exacerbated, the government is likely to control production capacity directly through state ownership.

While the above arguments capture the intrinsic difficulty of taxation in developing countries, they offer few insights into the government's purposes in collecting taxes and why the government would not create a policy environment that allows informal sectors to grow into formal sectors so as to enlarge the tax base. In this book, I have proposed an alternative explanation for the root cause and internal logic of the complicated interventionist policies in developing countries. Motivated by the dream of modernisation, nation building and gaining political as well as economic independence, most developing countries' governments – socialist and non-socialist alike – adopted various measures that attempted to accelerate the development of their then advanced capital-intensive industries after the Second World War. An economy's optimal industrial structure is, however, determined endogenously by its endowment structure (Lin and Zhang, 2007). The firms in the government's priority industries are not viable in an open, competitive market because these industries do not match the comparative advantage of the particular economy. As such, it is imperative for the government to introduce a series of regulations and interventions in international trade, the financial sector, the labour market and so on in order to mobilise the resources necessary for setting up and supporting the continuous operation of non-viable firms. This kind of development mode – in which the economic institutions are distorted as a coherent whole with its own inherent logic, necessary components and natural interaction of these components (Ericson, 1991; Kornai, 1992) – could be found in China and other Soviet-type economies before their transition to market economies in the 1980s or 1990s, and to a lesser extent in many other developing countries after the Second World War. This type of economy might be good at mobilising scarce resources and concentrating on a few clear, well-defined priority sectors (Ericson, 1991), but it will prove detrimental economy-wide (Sah and Stiglitz, 1987b) and will be highly costly for long-run growth (Acemoglu, Aghion and Zilibotti, 2006).

This appendix attempts to model the intrinsic logic of various institutional arrangements in a three-sector model with consideration of a government pursuing a CAD strategy. The inefficient regulations and distortions in the model resemble those inefficient institutions outlined by Acemoglu (2007b). Whereas Acemoglu's model emphasised the elite's use of political power to institute policies that increase their income through the transfer of resources, directly or indirectly, from the rest of the society to themselves, I emphasise the government's aim of building up advanced sectors in the early stages of development, which is driven by the benevolent purpose of nation building.

The remainder of the appendix is organised as follows. Section 2 presents the basic economic model and characterises equilibrium without governmental distortion – that is, under laissez-faire. Section 3 extends the basic model to analyse the formation of distorted prices for products and essential factors of production, highly centralised, planned resource allocation systems and a micromanagement mechanism in which firms have no autonomy. Section 4 provides the concluding remarks.

A1.2   The basic model

A1.2.1   Model set-up

The analysis in this appendix is based on a simple three-sector model of a dual economy. I consider a small developing country that trades three final goods – rural goods, labour-intensive industrial goods and capital-intensive industrial goods – at exogenously given world prices. These exogenously given world prices (shadow prices) for rural goods, labour-intensive goods and capital-intensive goods are p_a, p_l and p_c, respectively. I assume that rural goods and labour-intensive goods can be used only for consumption, while capital-intensive goods can be used only for investment.[2] Consumption goods are assumed to be normal.

In the rural sector, natural resources (rural land) and rural labour are combined to produce rural output. The rural production function, which exhibits constant returns to scale, is $Y_a = F(T,H^1)$. The variables Y_a, T and H^1 refer to rural output produced, total natural resources – which are owned within the rural sector – and total rural labour employed in the sector, a. As in Sah and Stiglitz (1984), the role of incentives in the rural sector is also emphasised in my model.[3] I assume the rural sector's population to be N^1 thus, $H^1/N^1 \equiv h^1$ denotes the hours worked by each rural worker and $T/N^1 \equiv t$ denotes the natural resources per rural worker. I denote a rural worker's consumption of rural and labour-intensive goods as (c_a^1, c_l^1). The surplus of the rural good per rural worker is given by $SF \equiv (t,h^1) - c_a^1$. The utility function and budget constraint of a rural worker are represented by $U^1 = U(c_a^1, c_l^1, h^1)$ and $p_a S \geq p_l c_l^1$ respectively.

The urban population is N^2, and an urban worker supplies h^2 hours of work inelastically. I normalise $h^2 = 1$ for simplicity; therefore, the

---

[2] I ignore the possibility of labour-intensive industrial goods being used for consumption and investment to avoid undue complexity, but the model in this appendix could easily be expanded to include this possibility.

[3] I emphasise the role of incentives in production teams in the rural sector (Lin, 1990) owing to the difficulty of supervising rural work.

total urban labour supply in this developing country is equal to the urban population – that is, $H^2 \equiv N^2$. I denote an urban worker's consumption of rural and labour-intensive goods as (c_a^2, c_l^2). The utility function and budget constraint of an urban worker are given by $U^2 = U(c_a^2, c_l^2)$ and $p_a c_a^2 + p_l c_l^2 \leq w$, respectively, where w is the wage of an urban worker per hour.

Capital and urban labour are combined to produce industrial output in the labour-intensive and capital-intensive sectors. The total capital stock in the developing country is $\overline{K}$, and $k \equiv \overline{K}/N^2$ is capital stock per urban worker. The production function for the labour-intensive sector, l, is as follows:

$$Y_l = A_l K_l^\beta H_l^{1-\beta} \qquad (A1.1)$$

Production of capital-intensive products requires a fixed input of $(1 - \delta)\Gamma$ units of capital-intensive goods[4] – that is, it requires paying a sunk entry cost, $(1 - \delta)\Gamma$, where δ represents a constant rate of depreciation, and Γ represents the initial investment. This satisfies $\delta \in (0,1)$, and then allows variable input – that is, capital and urban labour – to produce final output according to the following production function:

$$Y_c = A_c K_c^\alpha H_c^{1-\alpha} \qquad (A1.2)$$

Here, the subscript l denotes the labour-intensive sector and c denotes the capital-intensive sector. Because sector c is more capital-intensive than sector l, we have $\alpha > \beta$. The variables A_j, Y_j, K_j and H_j refer to total factor productivity, output produced, capital and

---

[4] I introduce the fixed input or sunk entry cost $(1 - \delta)\Gamma$ in the process of producing capital-intensive goods to reflect the basic characteristics of heavy industry in developing countries at their early stage of development, as summarised in Lin, Cai and Li (2003). One source of the fixed cost is the time and resources spent on learning the technology from the developed country. The larger the technology gap between the developing countries and the developed country the larger the cost. The other source of the fixed cost for a capital-intensive firm in the developing country is the need to invest in the production of most non-key components as well as key components by the firm itself, whereas the firm in a developed country could outsource most non-key components to other firms in the economy. The sunk entry cost $(1 - \delta)\Gamma$ could reflect the additional investment in production capacity for non-key components.

urban labour employed in sector $j = l, c$. The Cobb–Douglas form of production functions is adopted for tractability.

For analytical convenience, as in Hansen and Prescott (2002), I also assume that firms operating in each sector are competitive – that is, the firms in sector $j = l, c$ are price takers – and I also assume that there is at most one firm (if this firm is viable) in each sector. As in Shleifer and Vishny (1994), I assume that σ_j of the firm's profits, π_j, is owned by the manager, m_j, and fraction $1 - \sigma_j$ is owned by the treasury, which is assumed to be passive in this appendix, where $j = l, c$.[5] For the sake of simplicity, I do not distinguish between the manager and the shareholders of the firm, because I assume that the manager and the shareholders share common interests. I also assume that the labour-intensive firm's manager, m_l, and the capital-intensive firm's manager, m_c, are risk-neutral; therefore, the utility function of the manager, m_l, can be expressed by $U_{m_l} = \sigma_l \pi_l$. The utility function of the manager, m_c, is expressed by $U_{m_c} = \sigma_c \pi_c$.

A1.2.2 *Competitive equilibrium without government intervention*

Throughout this appendix, I consider a developing country whose capital stock per urban worker equals $\delta \underline{k}$, and $\underline{k}$ is a constant, which satisfies

$$\underline{k} = \left[\frac{p_c A_c}{p_l A_l} \left(\frac{1 - \alpha}{1 - \beta} \right)^{1 - \alpha} \left(\frac{\alpha}{\beta} \right)^{\alpha} \right]^{\frac{1}{\beta - \alpha}} {}^{6}$$

Given rural population N^1, urban population N^2, natural resources per rural worker t, working hours of urban labour $h^2 \equiv 1$ and total capital stock $\overline{K}$ in this developing country, and the exogenously given world prices (shadow prices) for rural goods p_a, labour-intensive

---

[5] In the model, σ_j describes the ownership of cash flows of the firm, which is close to zero in a publicly owned firm and close to one in a private firm.

[6] In the model, the extent of the scarcity in capital endowment in the developing country is an increasing function of $\delta \in (0, 1)$.

goods p_l and capital-intensive goods p_c, a competitive equilibrium without government intervention consists of a combination of the firm's allocations $\{K_l, L_l, K_c, H_c\}$, rural worker's allocations $\{c_a^1, c_l^1, h^1\}$, urban worker's allocations $\{c_a^2, c_l^2\}$, a tuple of the net exports of rural goods, labour-intensive goods and capital-intensive goods $\{E_a, E_l, E_c\}$, a (nominal) wage rate w for urban labour, and a (nominal) rental rate r for capital, such that the following conditions are satisfied.

(1) Given output prices and factor prices $\{p_a, p_l, p_c, w, r\}$, the j firm's allocation $\{K_j, L_j\}$ solves the following profit maximisation problem:

$$\max_{K_j, L_j} \pi_j \tag{A1.3}$$

where

$$\pi_l = p_l A_l K_l^\beta H_l^{1-\beta} - rK_l - wH_l$$

and

$$\pi_c = p_c[A_c K_c^\alpha H_c^{1-\alpha} - (1-\delta)\Gamma] - rK_c - wH_c$$

(2) Given the output prices and wage rate for the urban worker $\{p_a, p_l, w\}$, the rural worker's allocations maximise $U^1 = U$ (c_a^1, c_l^1, h^1) subject to $p_a S \geq p_l c_l^1$, and the urban worker's allocations maximise $U^2 = U(c_a^2, c_l^2)$ subject to $p_a c_a^2 + p_l c_l^2 \leq wh^2$.

(3) Markets clear:

$$K_l + K_c = \overline{K}$$

$$H_l + H_c = H^2$$

$$N^1 S = N^2 c_a^2 + E_a$$

$$q_l = N^1 c_l^1 + N^2 c_l^2 + E_l$$

(4) Trade balance:

$$p_a E_a + p_l E_l + p_c E_c = 0$$

(5) Investment equation:

$$I = \begin{cases} -E_c + q_c - (1-\delta)\Gamma, & \text{if} \quad q_c - (1-\delta)\Gamma > 0 \\ -E_c, & \text{if} \quad q_c(1-\delta)\Gamma \leq 0 \end{cases}$$

Given output prices (p_l, p_c) and factor prices (w, r), the cost function of the labour-intensive firm is $\varphi_l(q_l) = q_l/A_l(w/1-\beta)^{1-\beta}(r/\beta)^\beta$, and the variable cost function of the capital-intensive firm is $\varphi_c(q_c) = q_c/A_c(w/1-\alpha)^{1-\alpha}(r/\alpha)^\alpha,$[7] where q_l and q_c are the outputs produced by the labour-intensive firm and the capital-intensive firm respectively. Summarising the analysis above, I have the following proposition.

Proposition 1   For a developing country whose capital stock per urban worker equals $k = \delta k$, the capital-intensive firm would have incurred a loss if it had been set up and operated;[8] therefore, only the labour-intensive firm is operated in this developing country.

Proof   Given output prices $\{p_l, p_c\}$, the diversification cone of production functions $Y_l = A_l K_l^\beta H_l^{1-\beta}$ and $Y_c = A_c K_c^\alpha H_c^{1-\alpha}$ is $\underline{k}, \overline{k}$, where

$$\overline{k} = \left[\frac{p_c A_c}{p_l A_l} \left(\frac{1-\alpha}{1-\beta} \right)^{1-\beta} \left(\frac{\alpha}{\beta} \right)^\beta \right]^{\frac{1}{\beta-\alpha}}$$

Therefore, the capital-intensive production process would not be operated in a developing country whose capital stock per urban worker equalled $k = \delta k$, even without the fixed costs $(1-\delta)\Gamma p_c$; only the labour-intensive firm is operated in this developing country.

QED.

---

[7] The form of the total cost function of the capital-intensive firm in this appendix resembles that in Bernard, Rodding and Schott (2007).

[8] It could be argued that a firm is non-viable when it incurs a net loss in this appendix.

From proposition 1, we know that the equilibrium (real) wage and (real) rental rate of capital when labour-intensive good is used as numeraire[9] in the developing country are

$$\frac{r^*}{p_l} = A_l \beta k^{\beta - 1} \tag{A1.4}$$

$$\frac{w^*}{p_l} = A_l (1 - \beta) k^{\beta} \tag{A1.5}$$

The utility of manager m_l is $U_{m_l} = 0$, and the utility of manager m_c is $U_{m_c} = 0$. In fact, we can denote the reservation utility of manager m_l and manager m_c as $U_{m_l} = 0$ and $U_{m_c} = 0$, respectively.

The indirect utility function of the rural worker is obtained from

$$V^1(p_a/p_l, t) = \max_{c_a^1, c_l^1, h^1} U(c_a^1, c_l^1, h^1) + \lambda^1 \left\{ \frac{p_a}{p_l}[F(t, h^1) - c_a] - c_l^1 \right\}$$

where λ^1 is the rural worker's positive marginal utility of (real) income. From the envelope, we have $\partial V^1/\partial(p_a/p_l) = \lambda^1 S > 0$, which means that the rural worker's utility is an increasing function of rural output price p_a and a decreasing function of labour-intensive output price p_l. I assume that there is a lower bound value p_{al} for the relative price of rural products to labour-intensive products p_a/p_l such that $V^1(p_{al}, t) = \overline{V}^1$, where $\overline{V}^1$ is the subsistence level for the rural worker. In other words, I assume an agricultural crisis would occur if the relative price of a rural product to a labour-intensive product were less than the threshold value p_{al}, which would reduce the farmer's incentive to produce agricultural products.[10]

The indirect utility function of the urban worker is obtained from

$$V^2(p_a/p_l, w/p_l) = \max_{c_a^2, c_l^2} U(c_a^2, c_l^2) + \lambda^2 \left[\frac{w}{p_l} - \frac{p_a}{p_l} c_a^2 - c_l^2 \right]$$

where λ^2 is the urban worker's positive marginal utility of real income. From the envelope theorem, I have $\partial V^2/\partial(w/p_l) = \lambda^2 > 0$

---

[9] The labour-intensive good is set as numeraire in the model.
[10] See Lin (1990) as well as Lin and Yang (2000) for details of China's agricultural crisis and the Chinese famine in 1959–61. In fact, the problem of apparent food shortages

and $\partial V^2/\partial(p_a/p_l) = -\lambda^2 c_a^2 < 0$, which means that the urban worker's utility is an increasing function of the real wage rate w/p_l and a decreasing function of the relative price of a rural product to a labour-intensive product p_a/p_l. I also assume that, for a given relative price of a rural product to a labour-intensive product p_{al}, there exists a threshold value, $\underline{w_l}$, for the real wage rate w/p_l such that $V^2(\underline{p_{al}},\underline{w_l}) = \overline{V^2}$, where $\overline{V^2}$ is the subsistence level for the urban worker. The minimum real wage in the developing country, therefore, should not be less than $\underline{w_l}$, or else the urban worker could not afford to buy adequate rural products and/or labour-intensive goods.

The additive Bergson–Samuelson social welfare function is given by

$$\psi = N^1 W^1[V^1(p_a/p_l,t)] + N^2 W^2[V^2(p_a/p_l,w/p_l)] \quad \text{(A1.6)}$$

where $W^i(.)$ is a concave and increasing function of $V^i(.)$, $i = 1,2$. The amount of investment in this developing country without government intervention is

$$I = \frac{1}{p_c}\{p_a[N^1 F(t,h^1) - N^1 c_a^1 - N^2 c_a^2] + p_l(A_l H^2 k^\beta - N^1 c_l^1 - N^2 c_l^2)\}$$

From the analysis above, it is obvious that, given that resources are allocated by the market mechanism, producers will decide what to produce according to market prices of outputs and factors, and they will not produce capital-intensive goods in a developing country whose capital stock per urban worker equals $k \equiv \delta \underline{k}$. Consequently, if resources were allocated by the market mechanism, capital would not flow to the capital-intensive heavy industry sector. Rather, industrialisation featuring light industry would occur, which would be contrary to the goal of implementing a catch-up type of CAD heavy-industry-oriented development strategy in the developing countries. Therefore, without a cluster of intervention

emerged acutely and visibly in India in the late 1950s, and was experienced elsewhere as well (Krueger, 1995).

policies being enforced, the government in the developing country could not successfully enforce the catch-up type of CAD strategy.

A1.3 The trinity of economic institutions under a CAD strategy

Now I analyse the intrinsic logic of government intervention policies in the developing countries and how these are generated by a catch-up type of CAD strategy. For this reason, I define the utility function of the government (politicians) in developing countries. Suppose that the government in a developing country benefits from adopting a catch-up type of CAD strategy – that is, the government g in the developing country could gain utility $B(q_c)$ from the output of capital-intensive product q_c produced in that country, where $B(q_c)$ is twice continuously differentiable, with $B'(q_c) > 0$ and $B''(q_c) < 0$ for all $q_c > 0$ as well as $\lim_{q_c \to 0^+} B'(q_c) = \infty$. I assume that the utility function of the government, g, in the developing country is given by $U_g = \psi + \rho I + B(q_c)$, where I is investment in the developing country, ρ denotes the marginal social value of the investment and ψ is given by (A1.6).[11]

A1.3.1 Distorting relative prices

Output price distortion

In order to set up heavy industry projects, the government in the developing country could rely on collecting taxes from the rural and

---

[11] In the above utility function of the developing country government, U_g, $\psi + \rho I$ is borrowed from Sah and Stiglitz (1987a), and $B(q_c)$ is similar in form to B_i in Shleifer and Vishny (1994). The utility function used in this appendix, however, emphasises the strong motivation of the developing country government to reach a higher level of industrialisation and to leap over some economic development phases by taking capital-intensive (heavy) industries or import substitution as a basic development path after achieving political independence, which is neglected in Sah and Stiglitz (1987a). Unlike in Shleifer and Vishny (1994), the developing country government in this appendix is benevolent, not leviathan.

labour-intensive sectors to subsidise the capital-intensive sector.[12] I denote the tax rates in the rural sector and the labour-intensive sector to be τ_a and τ_l, respectively, and the subsidy rate in the capital-intensive sector to be τ_c. Now the prices in the rural, labour-intensive and capital-intensive sectors are $p_a - \tau_a$, $p_l - \tau_l$ and $p_c + \tau_c$, respectively. The total tax revenue raised from the rural and labour-intensive sectors is denoted as $\mathfrak{R}_a$ and $\mathfrak{R}_l$, respectively, and the total subsidy to the capital-intensive sector is denoted as $\mathfrak{R}_c$. As in Acemoglu (2007b), I also introduce two parameters $\phi_j \in [0,1]$ to measure how much of the tax revenue raised from sector $j = a,l$ can be redistributed to the capital-intensive sector.[13] Now the treasury's budget constraint is $\phi_a \mathfrak{R}_a + \phi_l \mathfrak{R}_l + (1 - \sigma_l)\pi_l + (1 - \sigma_c)\pi_c \geq \mathfrak{R}_c$.

I assume that $\phi_a = 0$ to reflect the fact that collecting tax from the small and scattered rural sector in the developing country is so difficult and costly that all tax revenue just covers the cost of collecting tax.[14] Now the treasury's budget constraint is given by

$$\phi_l \tau_l q_l + (1 - \sigma_l)\pi_l + (1 - \sigma_c)\pi_c \geq \tau_c q_c \qquad (A1.7)$$

Given output prices $\{(p_l - \tau_l),(p_c + \tau_c)\}$, now the diversification cone of labour-intensive and capital-intensive production functions is $[\Delta \underline{k}, \Delta \overline{k}]$, where

$$\Delta \equiv \left[\frac{(p_l - \tau_l)p_c}{(p_c + \tau_c)p_l} \right]^{\frac{1}{\alpha - \beta}}$$

After output price distortion, when $k < \Delta k$, the capital-intensive firm, c, will still not be able to survive,[15] and $U_{m_c} < 0$, provided

---

[12] I assume that there are no non-distortionary lump sum taxes available in the developing country.

[13] The parameter $\varphi \in [0,1]$ in Acemoglu (2007b) captures 'state capacity' – that is, the state's ability to penetrate and regulate production relations in a society, while, in this appendix , $\varphi_j \in [0,1]$ is interpreted as the state's efficiency in collecting tax from sector.

[14] I assume $\varphi_a \in (0,1]$ to avoid undue complexity; even the main results in this appendix hold.

[15] I define 'survivability' as a firm's ability to survive in an open, competitive market. With the government's subsidisation and/or protection, a non-viable firm could

$q_c > 0$. When $k > \Delta\bar{k}$, the labour-intensive firm, will not survive, and $U_{m_l} < 0$, provided $q_l > 0$. Summarising the analysis above gives the following lemma.

Lemma 1 As long as the capital-intensive production process is operated, output prices after distortion should guarantee that the factor endowments in the developing country belong to the new diversification cone $[\Delta\underline{k},\Delta\bar{k}]$ – that is, $k \in (\Delta\underline{k},\Delta\bar{k})$, which means

$$\Delta < \delta < \frac{1 - \beta\alpha}{1 - \alpha\beta}\Delta \qquad (A1.8)$$

From expression (A1.8) we know that, as long as the capital-intensive firm is operated, we must have $\tau_l > 0$ and $\tau_c > 0$. Thus, at the root of output price distortion in this appendix is the developing country government's pursuit of a catch-up type of CAD strategy – that is, taxing labour-intensive firms to subsidise and set up capital-intensive firms.

Depressing factor prices

Given the distorted output prices $(p_c + \tau_c, p_l - \tau_l)$, the market-clearing equilibrium (if equilibrium exists) wage and rental rate of capital in the developing country when the capital-intensive firm is operated must be

$$r' = (p_c + \tau_c)A_c\alpha(K'_c)^{\alpha-1}(H'_c)^{1-\alpha} = (p_l - \tau_l)A_l\beta(K'_l)^{\beta-1}(H'_l)^{1-\beta} \qquad (A1.9)$$

$$w' = (p_c + \tau_c)A_c(1 - \alpha)(K'_c)^{\alpha}(H'_c)^{-\alpha} = (p_l - \tau_l)A_l(1 - \beta)(K'_l)^{\beta}(H'_l)^{-\beta} \qquad (A1.10)$$

where K'_j and H'_j are capital and urban labour used in the firm $j = l,c$, respectively, after output price distortion.[16]

Footnote no. 15 (cont.)
survive. Similarly, a viable firm might not survive if the government's tax is too heavy.
[16] When producing capital-intensive products that do not require fixed input – that is, when $\Gamma = 0$ or $\delta = 1$ – the wage rate w and interest rate r are the market-clearing equilibrium factor prices, and K'_j and H'_j are market-clearing equilibrium capital and urban

Comparing the equilibrium real wage rate w^*/p_l and real interest rate r^*/p_l before output price distortion with the market-clearing equilibrium (if equilibrium exists) real wage rate $w'/(p_l - \tau_l)$, which is determined by (A1.10), and the real interest rate $r'/(p_l - \tau_l)$, which is determined by (A1.9) after output price distortion, yields the following lemma.

Lemma 2 Whenever the capital-intensive sector is operated in the developing country, the market-clearing equilibrium (if equilibrium exists) real wage rate (labour-intensive good as the numeraire), $w'/(p_l - \tau_l)$, after output price distortion must be less than the equilibrium real wage rate w^*/p_l without distortion. The market-clearing equilibrium (if equilibrium exists) real interest rate $r'/(p_l - \tau_l)$ after output price distortion must be greater than the equilibrium real interest rate r^*/p_l without distortion.

Proof Substituting (A1.5) into (A1.10), we obtain

$$\frac{w^*/p_l}{w'/(p_l - \tau_l)} = \left[\frac{k}{K_l/H_l}\right]^\beta$$

And $w^*/p_l > w'/p_l - \tau_l$ follows from $K_l/H_l < k < K_c/H_c$ as long as the capital-intensive sector is operated. Substituting (A1.4) into (A1.9), we obtain

$$\frac{r'/(p_l - \tau_l)}{r^*/p_l} = \left[\frac{k}{K_l/H_l}\right]^{1-\beta}$$

For the same reason, we have $r'/p_l - \tau_l > r^*/p_l$.

QED.

Given the distorted output prices $(p_c + \tau_c, p_l - \tau_l)$ and the market-clearing equilibrium real wage rate $w'/(p_l - \tau_l)$, which is determined by (A1.10), and real interest rate $r'/(p_l - \tau_l)$, which is determined by (A1.9), from Euler's theorem on homogeneous functions, we

labour used in the firm $j = l, c$, respectively, after output price distortion, which guarantees that the factor endowments in the developing country belong to the new diversification cone $[\Delta \underline{k}, \Delta \overline{k}]$.

know that the capital-intensive firm would incur a net loss of $(p_c + \tau_c)(1 - \delta)\Gamma$ and thus would not survive, no matter how much τ_c and τ_l are. The net loss, $(p_c + \tau_c)(1 - \delta)\Gamma$, is a decreasing function of the capital stock per urban worker, $k = \delta\underline{k}$.[17] The analysis above gives the following result.

Proposition 2   A developing country government could not implement a catch-up type of CAD strategy successfully just by a single policy instrument of distorting output prices. Therefore, the developing country government is obliged to manipulate factor prices as well as distort output prices to implement a catch-up type of CAD strategy successfully – that is, in addition to distorting output prices, the government has no choice but to reduce interest rates or keep the nominal wage rate down, or depress both, to implement a catch-up type of CAD strategy successfully.

I focus here on the role of a low interest rate policy in a developing country's implementation of a catch-up type of CAD strategy in accordance with widespread financial repression existing in the developing country, and investigate how a low interest rate policy can arise from the CAD strategy. To show this, first I need to specify the mechanism for urban wage determination.

Given the distorted relative prices of outputs $\{(p_a - \tau_a),$ $(p_l - \tau_l),(p_c + \tau_c)\}$, I denote the manipulated wage and rental rate of capital in the developing country as w_d and r_d, respectively. The indirect utility function of the urban worker after output price distortion and factor price manipulation is obtained from

$$V^2\left(\frac{p_a - \tau_a}{p_l - \tau_l}, \frac{w_d}{p_l - \tau_l}\right) = \max_{c_a^2, c_l^2} U(c_a^2, c_l^2) + \lambda^2\left[\frac{w_d}{p_l - \tau_l} - \frac{p_a - \tau_a}{p_l - \tau_l}c_a^2 - c_l^2\right]$$

[17] Owing to the fact that the capital-intensive firm still could not survive after the output price distortion without factor price manipulation, the market-clearing equilibrium wage and rental rates in the developing country are still determined by $w^{**} = (p_l - \tau_l)A_l(1 - \beta)k^\beta$ and $r^{**} = (p_l - \tau_l)A_l\beta k^{\beta-1}$ respectively.

where λ^2 is the urban worker's positive marginal utility of real income. I assume that the government in the developing country can exercise direct control of the urban wage only when the real wage rate of urban workers is above subsistence levels. When the real wage rate of urban workers equals the subsistence level, the government could not reduce urban workers' real wage further arbitrarily[18] – otherwise, in order to compensate for the loss of the urban workers' utility, the government would be obliged to depress the relative price of rural products to labour-intensive products.[19] The lower bound value $\underline{p_{al}}$ for the relative price of rural products to labour-intensive products assumed above implies that, with the purpose of maintaining the utility of urban workers above their subsistence levels, the minimum real wage rate should be no less than $\underline{w_l}$, which satisfies $V^2(\underline{p_{al}},\underline{w_l}) = \overline{V^2}$.

Let us assume that urban population and capital stock $\overline{K}$ in the developing country, productivity parameters (A_c,A_l), fixed input Γ, the subsistence level for urban workers and rural workers (V^1,V^2), the lower bound value $\underline{p_{al}}$ for the relative price of rural products to labour-intensive products, the minimum (real) wage in the developing country $\underline{w_l}$ and exogenous parameters (α,β,δ) in the developing country satisfy the following assumption: in order to guarantee that

---

[18] In Sah and Stiglitz (1987a), the government in a socialist economy can exercise direct control of urban wages without consideration of the urban workers' welfare, while, in a mixed (non-socialist) economy, the urban wage is determined from $V^2(p,w) = \overline{V^2}$ – that is, the urban wage will be adjusted in the face of changing prices to preserve the welfare of urban workers, and the government in a mixed economy has no right to exercise direct control of urban wages. Even in a socialist, planned economy, the government still has an obligation to urban workers' survival by guaranteeing them enough food and living necessities. This is the reason why, during the agricultural crisis in China in 1959–61, the famine existed in rural areas instead of urban areas (Lin and Yang, 2000).

[19] Though the assumption of $\varphi_a = 0$ implies that a developing country cannot collect tax directly from the rural sector to subsidise the capital-intensive sector, the government still wants to lower the price of rural products to compensate for the loss of urban workers' welfare. Thus, a large proportion of the costs of heavy industry development, through such a mechanism, were transferred implicitly to traditional economic sectors such as agriculture (Lin, Cai and Li, 2003).

the capital-intensive firm survives, the government needs to distort the relative prices of labour-intensive products to capital-intensive products to such an extent that

$$\frac{w'}{(p_l - \tau_l)} < \underline{w}_l \qquad\qquad \text{(A1.A)}$$

where $w'/(p_l - \tau_l)$ is determined by (A1.10), which is the market-clearing equilibrium (if equilibrium exists) real wage in the developing country when the capital-intensive firm is operated.

Consequently, depending on whether assumption (A1.A) holds, the government might or might not be able to exercise direct control of urban wages at will. When assumption (A1.A) holds, the government cannot exercise direct control of urban wages arbitrarily after distorting relative prices of outputs $\{(p_a - \tau_a),(p_l - \tau_l),(p_c + \tau_c)\}$; therefore, the urban wage encountered by labour-intensive and capital-intensive firms is $w_d \equiv \underline{w}_l(p_l - \tau_l)$.[20] Throughout, I presume that assumption (A1.A) holds, which ensures the necessity of further depressing the interest rates affecting capital-intensive firms in order for the government to implement a catch-up type of CAD strategy successfully, and I denote the interest rates affecting the capital-intensive and the labour-intensive firms as r_d^c and r_d^l respectively. Considering that low interest rates would reduce the supply of capital – thereby decreasing the availability of capital in the developing country – I assume that the (nominal) interest rate faced by firm $j = l, c$ should be no less than $v_j r^*$, where v_j is an exogenously given positive parameter; thus, we have $v_j r^* \leq r_d^j$.

Given distorted relative prices of outputs $\{(p_l - \tau_l),(p_c + \tau_c)\}$ and depressed factor prices $\{w_d, r_d^c\}$, the profit function of the capital-intensive firm is

$$\pi_c(p_c, \tau_c, r_d^c, w_d) = \qquad\qquad \text{(A1.11)}$$

[20] Depending on whether assumption (A1.A) holds, there is a possibility of excess demand or excess supply of urban workers in this developing country. When assumption (A1.A) holds, the redundant employment in the urban sector would result endogenously from the government's pursuit of a catch-up type of CAD strategy.

$$\text{Max}\left\{\max_{K_c,H_c}(p_c+\tau_c)[A_c(K_c)^\alpha(H_c)^{1-\alpha}-(1-\delta)\Gamma]-r^c_dK_c-w_dH_c,0\right\}$$

The above capital-intensive firm's profit maximisation implies that the amount of capital and labour used in this firm must satisfy

$$(p_c+\tau_c)A_c\alpha(K_c)^{\alpha-1}(H_c)^{1-\alpha}\geq r^c_d \text{ or } (p_c+\tau_c)A_c$$
$$(1-\alpha)(K_c)^\alpha(H_c)^{-\alpha}\geq w_d \qquad \text{(A1.12)}$$

with at least one strict inequality in (A1.12). $(p_c+\tau_c)A_c(1-\alpha)$ $(K_c)^\alpha(H_c)^{-\alpha}>w_d$ is impossible, however, according to assumption (A1.A). Thus we have $(p_c+\tau_c)A_c\alpha(K_c)^{\alpha-1}(H_c)^{1-\alpha}>r^c_d$, which implies that we have $r^c_d<r'$. Summarising the analysis above gives the following result.

Proposition 3 In order to implement a catch-up type of CAD strategy successfully, the government of a developing country is obliged to depress the interest rate from r' to r^c_d as well as distorting output prices, and the depressed interest rate r^c_d (Aoos. should guarantee that the capital-intensive firm will survive – that is, the right-hand side in (A1.11) is non-negative.

A1.3.2 *The planned resource allocation system*

Following Bénassy (2008), in studying the non-clearing markets it is necessary to make an important distinction between demands of factors on the one hand and the resulting allocations of factors on the other. The demands of factors, denoted by $\tilde{n}_{ji}$, are signals of factor $i=H,K$ transmitted by firm $j=l,c$ to the government before exchange/allocation takes place.

Facing the distorted relative prices of outputs $\{(p_l-\tau_l),(p_c+\tau_c)\}$ and the depressed factor prices $\{w_d,r^c_d\}$, the capital-intensive firm's demands of factors $\tilde{n}_{ci}$ satisfy

$$(p_c+\tau_c)A_c\alpha(\tilde{n}_{cK})^{\alpha-1}(\tilde{n}_{cH})^{1-\alpha}=r^c_d$$
$$(p_c+\tau_c)A_c(1-\alpha)(\tilde{n}_{cK})^\alpha(\tilde{n}_{cK})^{-\alpha}=w_d$$

Because $r_d^c < r'$ and $w' < w_d$, we have $\tilde{n}_{cK} > K_c'$ and/or $\tilde{n}_{cH} < H_c'$, where K_c' and H_c' are determined by and simultaneously.

Given the distorted relative prices of outputs $\{(p_l - \tau_l), (p_c + \tau_c)\}$ and the depressed factor prices $\{w_d, r_d^l\}$, the profit function of the labour-intensive firm is

$$\pi_l(p_l, \tau_l, r_d^l, w_d) = \text{Max}\left\{ \max_{K_l, H_l} (p_l - \tau_l) A_l(K_l)^\beta (H_l)^{1-\beta} - r_d^l K_l - w_d H_l, 0 \right\}$$

The above labour-intensive firm's profit maximisation implies that the amount of capital and labour used in this firm must satisfy

$$(p_l - \tau_l) A_l \beta (K_l)^{\beta - 1}(H_l)^{1-\beta} \geq r_d^l \text{ or } (p_l - \tau_l) A_l (1 - \beta)$$
$$(K_l)^\beta (H_l)^{-\beta} \geq w_d$$

From assumption (A1.A), $(p_l - \tau_l) A_l (1 - \beta)(K_l)^\beta (H_l)^{-\beta} > w_d$ could not be true. Thus, we must have $r_d^l \leq r'$ as the result of $(p_l - \tau_l)$ $A_l \beta (K_l)^{\beta - 1}(H_l)^{1-\beta} \geq r_d^l$.

Facing the distorted relative prices of outputs $\{(p_l - \tau_l), (p_c + \tau_c)\}$ and the depressed factor prices $\{w_d, r_d^l\}$, the labour-intensive firm's demands of factors $\tilde{n}_{li}$ satisfy

$$(p_l - \tau_l) A_l \beta (\tilde{n}_{lK})^{\beta - 1}(\tilde{n}_{lH})^{1-\beta} = r_d^l$$

$$(p_l - \tau_l) A_l (1 - \beta)(\tilde{n}_{lK})^\beta (\tilde{n}_{lH})^{-\beta} = w_d$$

Owing to $r_d^l \leq r'$ and $w' < w_d$, we must have $\tilde{n}_{lK} \geq K_l'$ and/or $\tilde{n}_{lH} < H_l'$, where K_c' and H_c' are determined by and simultaneously.

Therefore, we must have $\tilde{n}_{cK} + \tilde{n}_{lK} > K_c' + K_l' \equiv \overline{K}$ and/or $\tilde{n}_{cH} + \tilde{n}_{lH} < H_c' + H_l' \equiv H^2$. Summarising the analysis above gives the following lemma.

Lemma 3 When assumption (A1.A) holds, a shortage of capital and/or a surplus of urban labour will be created in the developing country due to the introduction of a catch-up type of CAD strategy. Thus, some rationing will necessarily occur.[21]

As we know, the various forms of rationing include uniform rationing, queuing, priority systems and proportional rationing, depending on the particular organisation of each market (Bénassy, 2006). No matter what form the rationing takes, the resulting allocations, denoted by n_{ji}^*, are exchanges/allocations made by the developing country government, the allocation process must satisfy the resulting allocations and the factor supply, denoted by Z_i^*, must be identically balanced for each factor market $i = H,K$ – that is, $N_i^* = \Sigma(n_{li}^* + n_{ci}^*) = Z_i^*$ for $i = H,K$, where $Z_H^* \equiv H^2$ and $Z_K^* \equiv \overline{K}$.

Owing to the surplus of urban labour, labour-intensive or capital-intensive firms, or both, should be forced to employ more labour than what is demanded, which is expressed by

$$\tilde{n}_{lH} \leq n_{lH}^* \text{ and (or) } \tilde{n}_{cH} \leq n_{cH}^*$$

In this model, therefore, the form of rationing chosen by the developing country government violates the first property of rationing schemes in Bénassy (2008) – *voluntary exchange* in the labour market.

Furthermore, given distorted relative prices of outputs $\{(p_l - \tau_l),(p_c + \tau_c)\}$ and the resulting allocations of capital $n_{ji}^*(i = L,K)$ to firm $j = l,c$ by the developing country government, the marginal value product (MVP) of capital in the capital-intensive firm is

$$(p_c + \tau_c)A_c\alpha(n_{cK}^*)^{\alpha-1}(n_{cH}^*)^{1-\alpha} \tag{A1.13}$$

and the MVP of capital in the labour-intensive firm is

---

[21] Shleifer and Vishny (1992) present a new theory of pervasive shortages under socialism, based on the assumption that planners are self-interested, and provide an overview of the standard explanations of shortages of goods under socialism. These explanations do not, however, include my reasoning of shortages in developing countries, which is based on the governments' adoption of a catch-up type of CAD strategy.

$$(p_l - \tau_l)A_l\beta(n_{lK}^*)^{\beta-1}(n_{lH}^*)^{1-\beta} \qquad (A1.14)$$

As long as (A1.13) is not equal to (A1.14), there always exists a mutually advantageous exchange between labour-intensive and capital-intensive firms by transferring the capital allocated by the government from one firm to another. Consequently, in this model, the form of rationing chosen by the government might violate the second property of rationing schemes in Bénassy (2008) – *efficiency in the capital market*.

Considering that the rationing scheme adopted by the government does (might) not satisfy two properties in Bénassy (2008), we obtain the following proposition.

Proposition 4 When assumption (A1.A) holds, the successful implementation of a catch-up type of CAD strategy in a developing country implies that the only form of rationing that can be adopted by the government is allocating capital and urban labour to the labour-intensive and capital-intensive firms through priority systems.

In fact, resource allocation is extremely complex and difficult owing to the information asymmetry between the government and the firms. I assume that the factor markets were visited sequentially in an order that gave priority to capital-intensive firms and effective demands of factors $\tilde{n}_{ci}(i = L,K)$ were expressed by capital-intensive firms. After the resulting allocations of factors $n_{ci}^*(i = L,K)$ to capital-intensive firms had been realised, the remaining factors were allocated to labour-intensive firms, which means $n_{li}^* = Z_i^* - n_{ci}^*(i = L,K)$.[22]

Moreover, in view of the possibility of manager m_j transferring resources outside firm j to firm $-j$, it is necessary to make a critical distinction between the resulting allocations of factors to firm $j = l,c$, denoted by $n_{ji}^*(i = L,K)$, on the one hand and the equilibrium amount of factors used in firm j, denoted by $\tilde{n}_{ji}^*(i = L,K)$, on the other.

---

[22] The equilibrium of resource allocation with non-clearing markets in this appendix is reached through the non-tâtonnement process in Bénassy (1977).

The equilibrium amount of factors used in firm j is the quantity of factors finally used in firm j, where all economic forces are balanced, and, in the absence of external shocks, $\tilde{n}_{ji}^{*}$ will not change.

A1.3.3 *Depriving a firm of autonomy*

Under the conditions in which prices were distorted and factors were allocated to firms by the government through priority systems, profits and losses could no longer reflect management performance. Because of information asymmetry, the government's costs of monitoring managers were prohibitively high.[23] Thus, calculating how to guarantee the factors allocated by governments to be used in the priority sector – that is, in capital-intensive firms – and to avoid investment arbitrage is of vital importance to the government's successful implementation of a catch-up type of CAD strategy. As in the pioneering work of Grossman and Hart (1986), as well as Hart and Moore (1990), I assume that all the factors used in capital-intensive and labour-intensive firms are ex ante non-verifiable and non-contractible. In other words, I suppose that it is costly for the government and managers to write detailed long-term contracts that specify precisely the uses of factors allocated to firms by the government as a function of every possible eventuality and that, as a result, the contracts are incomplete (Hart and Moore, 1990). Therefore, the controlling right over the use of factors allocated by the developing country government, rather than the incentive contract, becomes the critical determinant of the equilibrium of resource allocation with non-clearing markets.

Following Shleifer and Vishny (1994), I distinguish firms based on who owns their cash flows (the treasury or manager m_{j} of firm $j = l,c$) and who has control rights of the use of factors (the government or manager m_{j}).[24] In terms of the model above, parameter σ_{j} describes

---

[23] In the present model, there will be no asymmetries of information between the government and managers.

[24] Grossman and Hart (1986) define that a firm consists of those assets that it owns or over which it has control. They do not distinguish between ownership and control and virtually define ownership as the power to exercise control.

the ownership of cash flows of firm $j = l,c$, while either the government or the managers can control the exact use of the resulting allocation of factors n_{ji}^*. The allocation of rights over cash flow and control in this model also has an economic interpretation like that in Shleifer and Vishny (1994), which means that, in a conventional state-owned enterprise, the government controls the exact use of the resulting allocations of factors n_{ji}^*, and the cash flow is owned mostly by the treasury (σ_j is low). What is more, the allocation of the control right in this model also has a new economic interpretation – that is, when the government has full control of the exact use of the allocations of factors n_{ji}^*, firms are deprived of autonomy in production and management.

In order to prove that the developing country government prefers to deprive a firm of autonomy, we need to compute the equilibrium of resource allocation with non-clearing markets where the manager and the government have the control rights, respectively, and then contrast these two equilibria. For the sake of the model's tractability, I assume that the resulting allocation of labour in the capital-intensive firm, n_{cH}^*, equals $\Xi \equiv H_c' + \varepsilon$, under government control and under manager control, and Ξ is an exogenously given constant for simplicity, where is a scalar – that is, we have $n_{cH}^* = \Xi$ for simplicity. Thus, the resulting allocation of labour in the labour-intensive firm, n_{lH}^*, equals $H^2 - \Xi$; in other words, $n_{lH}^* = H^2 - \Xi$. To highlight the mechanism of depriving a firm of autonomy in the simplest possible way, let us assume that managers cannot transfer labour outside from one firm to another.[25] Now the unresolved question is to determine who – the government or manager m_j – has the control right over the exact use of the resulting allocations of capital, n_{jK}^*, in firm $j = l,c$.

---

[25] This assumption might seem too extreme at first glance, but it could be true in some developing countries – such as China, which carries out strict personnel controls through a 'hukou' (census registry) institution.

Before proceeding to compute equilibrium, as a matter of convenience, I need once more to describe the utility function of the government in the developing country. Given the distorted output prices $(p_a - \tau_a, p_c + \tau_c, p_l - \tau_l)$ and the depressed wage rate $w_d \equiv w_l(p_l - \tau_l)$, the utility function of the government can be expressed by

$$U_g = \psi + \rho I + B(q_c) \qquad (A1.15)$$

where

$$\psi = N^1 W^1\left[V^1\left(\frac{p_a - \tau_a}{p_l - \tau_l}, t\right) \right] + N^2 W^2\left[V^2\left(\frac{p_a - \tau_a}{p_l - \tau_l}, \frac{w_d}{p_l - \tau_l}\right) \right]$$

$$V^1\left(\frac{p_a - \tau_a}{p_l - \tau_l}, t\right) = \max_{c_a^1, c_l^1, h^1} U(c_a^1, c_l^1, h^1) + \lambda^1\left\{\frac{p_a - \tau_a}{p_l - \tau_l}[F(t, h^1) - c_a^1] - c_l^1\right\}$$

$$V^2\left(\frac{p_a - \tau_a}{p_l - \tau_l}, \frac{w_d}{p_l - \tau_l}\right) = \max_{c_a^2, c_l^2} U(c_a^2, c_l^2) + \lambda^2\left[\frac{w_d}{p_l - \tau_l} - \frac{p_a - \tau_a}{p_l - \tau_l}c_a^2 - c_l^2\right]$$

$$I = \frac{p_l - \tau_l}{p_c + \tau_c}\left[\frac{p_a - \tau_a}{p_l - \tau_l}\{N^1[F(t, h^1) - c_a^1] - N^2 c_a^2\} + (q_l - N^1 c_l^1 - N^2 c_l^2)\right]$$
$$+ q_c - (1 - \delta)\Gamma$$

Furthermore, assumption (A1.A) implies that we have $(p_a - \tau_a)/(p_l - \tau_l) \equiv \underline{p}_{al}$ and $w_d/(p_l - \tau_l) \equiv w_l$ as well as

$$U_g = N^1 W^1(\overline{V}^1) + N^2 W^2(\overline{V}^2) + B(q_c) +$$

Thus, the utility function of the government can be expressed by

$$U_g = N^1 W^1(\overline{V}^1) + N^2 W^2(\overline{V}^2) + B(q_c) + \qquad A1.16$$

$$\rho\left\{\frac{p_l - \tau_l}{p_c + \tau_c}\left[\underline{p}_{al}\{N^1[F(t, h^1) - c_a^1] - N^2 c_a^2\} + (q_l - N^1 c_l^1 - N^2 c_l^2)\right]\right.$$
$$\left. + q_c - (1 - \delta)\Gamma\right\}$$

In the following subsections, I first compute equilibrium under government control – that is, the government has the control right over the exact use of the resulting allocations of capital, n_{jK}^*, in firm $j = l,c$ – then solve equilibrium under the manager's control – that is, manager m_j has the control right over the exact use of the resulting allocations of capital, n_{jK}^*, in firm j. Finally, I compare equilibrium under government control with that under manager control.

Equilibrium under government control

When the government in a developing country has the control right over the exact use of resulting allocations of capital, n_{jK}^*, in firm $j = l,c$, there is no possibility for manager m_j to transfer capital outside from firm j to firm $-j$; thus, we must have $\tilde{n}_{ji}^* \equiv n_{ji}^*$ – that is, the resulting allocations of factors to firm $j = l,c$ will always be equal to the equilibrium amount of factors used in that firm. In this way, the government can choose distorted output prices $(p_a - \tau_a, p_c + \tau_c, p_l - \tau_l)$, depressed interest rates (r_d^c, r_d^l) for capital-intensive and labour-intensive firms, respectively, and the resulting allocations of capital, n_{jK}^*, in firm j to maximise utility – which was expressed in (A1.16) subject to the treasury's budget constraint (A1.17) – as well as the constraints that manager m_j be kept to his/her reservation utility of zero: $U_{m_j} \equiv \sigma_j \pi_j \geq 0$.

Given distorted output prices $(p_c + \tau_c, p_l - \tau_l)$, depressed factor prices (r_d^c, r_d^l, w_d) and the resulting allocation of factors $n_{ji}^*(i = K, H)$ in firm $j = l,c$,[26] the utility of manager m_c is given by

$$U_{m_c} \equiv \sigma_c[(p_c + \tau_c)A_c(n_{cK}^*)^\alpha(\Xi)^{1-\alpha} - r_d^c n_{cK}^* \quad \text{(A1.17)}$$
$$- w_d\Xi - (p_c + \tau_c)(1 - \delta)\Gamma]$$

and the utility of manager m_l is given by

$$U_{m_l} \equiv \sigma_l[(p_l - \tau_l)A_l(n_{lK}^*)^\beta(H^2 - \Xi)^{1-\beta} - r_d^l n_{lK}^* - w_d(H^2 - \Xi)] \quad \text{(A1.18)}$$

[26] We have $n_{cH}^* = \Xi$ and $n_{lH}^* = H^2 - \Xi$ based on the assumption made above.

It is evident that the constraints that manager m_j be kept to his/her reservation utility of zero are binding, which implies that $\pi_j = 0$. As $\pi_j = 0$, the treasury's budget constraint can be expressed by

$$\phi_l \tau_l q_l \geq \tau_c q_c \qquad \text{(A1.19)}$$

The government's utility maximisation problem above can be solved as follows.

- Given output prices $(p_l - \tau_l, p_c + \tau_c)$, the resulting allocations n_{ji}^* and depressed wage rate w_d, the government in the developing country sets the depressed interest rate r_d^j affecting firm $j = l,c$ to maximise the profits of firm j. It is evident that the equilibrium interest rate r_d^{*jg} under government control in firm j equals $v_j r^* -$ that is, we have $r_d^{*jg} = v_j r^*$.
- Given the resulting allocations of labour to capital-intensive firm $n_{cH}^* = \Xi$ and the resulting allocations of labour to labour-intensive firm $n_{lH}^* = H^2 - \Xi$, if the equilibrium amount of capital used in the capital-intensive firm is n_{cK}^* then the equilibrium amount of capital used in the labour-intensive firm is $n_{lK}^* = \overline{K} - n_{cK}^*$ and the equilibrium output of labour-intensive and capital-intensive products produced in the developing country satisfy

$$q_l = A_l(\overline{K} - n_{cK}^*)^\beta (H^2 - \Xi)^{1-\beta} \quad and \quad q_c = A_c(n_{cK}^*)^\alpha \Xi^{1-\alpha} \qquad \text{(A1.20)}$$

- Plugging the equilibrium output of labour-intensive and capital-intensive products in (A1.20) into (A1.16), where $N^1 W^1(\overline{V}^1) + N^2 W^2(\overline{V}^2)$ is a constant and can be passed over, the utility function of the government in the developing country can be expressed by

$$\tilde{U}_g = B(A_c(n_{cK}^*)^\alpha \Xi^{1-\alpha}) + \rho\frac{p_l - \tau_l}{p_c + \tau_c}p_{al}\{N^1[F(t,h^1) - c_a^1] - N^2 c_a^2\} +$$

$$\rho\frac{p_l - \tau_l}{p_c + \tau_c}(A_l(\overline{K} - n_{cK}^*)^\beta (H^2 - \Xi)^{1-\beta} - N^1 c_l^1 - N^2 c_l^2) +$$

$$\rho[A_c(n^*_{cK})^\alpha \Xi^{1-\alpha} - (1-\delta)\Gamma]$$

- Finally, the government in the developing country chooses the distorted extent of relative prices of labour-intensive products to capital-intensive products $(p_l - \tau_l)/(p_c - \tau_c)$ and the resulting allocations of capital to capital-intensive firm n^*_{cK} to maximise $\bar{U}_g$, subject to the constraint that manager m_j be kept to his/her reservation utility of zero and the treasury's budget constraint, which can be expressed by

$$\phi_l \tau_l A_l (\overline{K} - n^*_{cK})^\beta (H^2 - \Xi)^{1-\beta} \geq \tau_c A_c (n^*_{cK})^\alpha \Xi^{1-\alpha}$$

Solving the government's utility maximisation problem yields the following first-order conditions:

$$-\frac{\rho}{p_c + \tau_c} p_{al}\{N^1[F(t,h^1) - c^1_a] - N^2 c^2_a\} + \qquad (A1.21)$$

$$\frac{-\rho}{p_c + \tau_c}(A_l(\overline{K} - n^*_{cK})^\beta (H^2 - \Xi)^{1-\beta} - N^1 c^1_l - N^2 c^2_l) +$$

$$\hbar^g \phi_l A_l (\overline{K} - n^*_{cK})^\beta (H^2 - \Xi)^{1-\beta} - e^g_l \sigma_l A_l (\overline{K} - n^*_{cK})^\beta (H^2 - \Xi)^{1-\beta} = 0$$

$$-\rho \frac{p_l - \tau_l}{(p_c + \tau_c)^2} p_{al}\{N^1[F(t,h^1) - c^1_a] - N^2 c^2_a\} +$$

$$-\rho \frac{p_l - \tau_l}{(p_c + \tau_c)^2}(A_l(\overline{K} - n^*_{cK})^\beta (H^2 - \Xi)^{1-\beta} - N^1 c^1_l - N^2 c^2_l)$$

$$\qquad (A1.22)$$

$$-\hbar^g A_c(n^*_{cK})^\alpha \Xi^{1-\alpha} + U^g_c \sigma_c[A_c(n^*_{cK})^\alpha (\Xi)^{1-\alpha} - (1-\delta)\Gamma] = 0$$

$$B'(A_c(n^*_{cK})^\alpha \Xi^{1-\alpha})A_c\alpha(n^*_{cK})^{\alpha-1}\Xi^{1-\alpha} +$$

$$-\rho \frac{p_l - \tau_l}{p_c + \tau_c}A_l\beta(\overline{K} - n^*_{cK})^{\beta-1}(H^2 - \Xi)^{1-\beta} + \rho A_c\alpha(n^*_{cK})^{\alpha-1}\Xi^{1-\alpha}$$

$$\qquad (A1.23)$$

$$+\hbar^g[-\phi_l \tau_l A_l\beta(\overline{K} - n^*_{cK})^{\beta-1}(H^2 - \Xi)^{1-\beta} - \tau_c A_c\alpha(n^*_{cK})^{\alpha-1}\Xi^{1-\alpha}]$$

$$+\chi^g_c \sigma_c[(p_c + \tau_c)A_c\alpha(n^*_{cK})^{\alpha-1}(\Xi)^{1-\alpha} - r^c_d]$$

$$+ \chi_l^g \sigma_l[- (p_l - \tau_l)A_l\beta(\overline{K} - n_{cK}^*)^{\beta-1}(H^2 - \Xi)^{1-\beta} + r_d^l] = 0$$

where $\hbar^g$, χ_c^g and χ_l^g are the Lagrange multipliers under government control for the treasury's budget constraint and the constraint that managers m_c and m_l are kept to their reservation utility of zero, respectively.

From the first-order conditions above, I can solve the equilibrium tax rate in labour-intensive firm τ_l^{*g}, the equilibrium subsidy rate in capital-intensive firm τ_c^{*g} and the resulting allocations of capital n_{jK}^{*g} in firm $j = l,c,$[27] which are equal to the equilibrium amount of capital used in that firm, $\tilde{n}_{jK}^{*g}$, under government control. The equilibrium tax rate in the rural sector, τ_a^{*g}, and the equilibrium (nominal) urban wage w_d^{*g} under government control are determined by

$$\tau_a^{*g} = p_a - p_{al}(p_l - \tau_l^{*g})$$

$$w_d^{*g} = w_l(p_l - \tau_l^{*g})$$

Finally, the other equilibrium endogenous variables under government control – for example, the equilibrium surplus of the rural good per rural worker S^{*g}, equilibrium investment I^{*g}, equilibrium output of capital-intensive product q_c^{*g} and equilibrium output of labour-intensive product q_l^{*g} under government control – can be determined after τ_a^{*g}, τ_l^{*g}, τ_c^{*g}, $\tilde{n}_{ji}^{*g}$, w_d^{*g} and r_d^{*jg} have been solved.

Moreover, the constraint that manager m_j is kept to his/her reservation utility of zero implies that I can replace Lagrange multipliers χ_c^g and χ_l^g in (A1.21), (A1.22) and (A1.23) with $\chi'^g_c = \chi_c^g \sigma_c$ and $\chi'^g_l = \chi_l^g \sigma_l$ without changing equilibrium under government control. Thus, we have the following proposition.

---

[27] Equilibrium under the circumstances is identical to the case of complete contracts for the government in the developing country (the 'first best' equilibrium from the government's point of view).

Proposition 5 Equilibrium with non-clearing markets under government control is independent of σ_j – that is, it is independent of the ownership of the firm's cash flow.[28]

Equilibrium under manager control

Now I need to compute equilibrium with non-clearing markets under manager m_j's control of the exact use of the resulting allocations of capital n_{jK}^* in firm j. Under manager control, as long as manager m_j has an incentive to transfer capital allocated by the government outside from firm j to firm $-j$, the resulting allocations of capital to firm $j = l,c$ could not be equal to the equilibrium amount of capital used in that firm – that is, $n_{jK}^* \neq \tilde{n}_{jK}^*$.

As in Shleifer and Vishny (1994), however, in this model the fact that manager m_j has the control right over the use of capital allocated by the government does not mean that the manager will transfer all the resources outside from firm j to firm $-j$. Indeed, the government could try to convince managers m_c and m_l to produce an acceptable quantity of capital-intensive products, q_c, and a desirable quantity of labour-intensive products, q_l, by means of changing the distorted extent of the relative output prices $(p_c + \tau_c)/(p_l - \tau_l)$, whereby the government might affect the relative return of capital between labour-intensive and capital-intensive firms. Therefore, based on the cooperative game theory, the government g, manager m_c and manager m_l could bargain for a superior allocation by producing an appropriate quantity of capital-intensive products and labour-intensive products and distorting the relative output prices $(p_c + \tau_c)/(p_l - \tau_l)$ to an appropriate extent simultaneously.

Following Hart and Moore (1990), in the model presented below I assume that the relationships among the government g, manager m_c

---

[28] Similar empirical results can be found in the paper by Morck and Yeung (2004), who emphasise that political influence is proportional to what one controls, not what one owns, notwithstanding the fact that the precise meaning of 'control' in this appendix is not identical to that in Morck and Yeung (2004).

and manager m_l could be described and analysed by an incomplete contract and I also assume that the ex post distribution of pay-off is governed by a (multilateral bargaining) coalitional game. The solution concept that I adopt for the coalitional game is the Shapley value (Shapley, 1953; see also Osborne and Rubinstein, 1994, and Winter, 2002).[29]

The chronology of all agents' main events and their decisions is shown as follows.

- The government distorts the relative output prices $(p_c + \tau_c)/(p_l - \tau_l)$ and gives priority to the capital-intensive firm by allocating capital with price r_d^c and urban labour with price w_d to this firm. The amount of capital and urban labour allocated to the capital-intensive firm is n_{cK}^* and $n_{cH}^* = \Xi$, respectively. After the resulting allocations of factors $n_{ci}^*(i = L,K)$ to the capital-intensive firm have been realised, the remaining factors with price r_d^l and w_d are allocated to the labour-intensive firm, which means that $n_{li}^* = Z_i^* - n_{ci}^*(i = L,K)$.

- Manager $j = l,c$ decides how much of the resulting allocations of capital will be diverted from firm j to firm $-j$. I denote the amount of the resulting allocations of capital diverted at χ. In fact, there are only two possible directions of capital transfer: from the capital-intensive firm to the labour-intensive firm or vice versa. If χ is permitted to be negative, the above decision problem of manager m_l and/or manager m_c will always be described equivalently, as manager m_c decides how much of the resulting allocations of capital will be diverted from his/her firm to the labour-intensive firm. When manager m_c has an incentive to transfer capital to a labour-intensive firm, we have $\chi > 0$, and when manager m_l has an incentive to transfer capital to a capital-intensive firm, we have $\chi < 0$. Thus, there is a wedge, denoted by

χ, between the equilibrium amount of capital used in the capital-intensive firm, denoted by $\tilde{n}^*_{cK}$, and the resulting allocations of capital, denoted by n^*_{cK}; in other words, $\tilde{n}^*_{cK} = n^*_{cK} - \chi$.

- The government, manager m_l and manager m_c decide on the division of the pay-off by a (multilateral bargaining) coalitional game.
- Output is produced and the pay-off is distributed according to their Shapley values.

I use a sub-game perfect equilibrium (SPE) to characterise the non-market-clearing-equilibrium under manager control, and the pay-offs distributed in all sub-games are determined by the Shapley values. Borrowing some notations used in Winter (2002), in the present model I can describe the coalitional game among the government g, manager m_c and manager m_l in an explicit way – that is, a coalitional game on a finite set of three players is a function, v, from the set of all $2^3 = 8$ coalitions to the set of real numbers with $v(\varnothing) = 0$. $v(S)$ represents the total pay-off that the coalitions, S, could get in the coalitional game, v. A value is an operator ϕ that assigns to each game v a vector of pay-offs, $\phi(v) = (\phi_g, \phi_{m_c}, \phi_{m_l})$ in $\square^3$. $\phi_\iota(v)$ stands for player ι's ($\iota = g, m_c, m_l$) pay-off in the game.

Each player ι's Shapley value is an operator that assigns the player the expected marginal contributions or the average contributions to all coalitions, S, that consist of players ($\iota = g, m_c, m_l$) ordered in all feasible permutations. More specifically, I denote Π to be a permutation of the set of players and $\overline{\Pi}$ to be the set of all feasible permutations. Let us imagine the players appearing one by one to collect their pay-off according to the order Π (Winter, 2002); then the marginal contribution of player ι with respect to that order, Π, is $v(\perp^\iota_\Pi \cup \iota) - v(\perp^\iota_\Pi)$ if I denote by $\perp^\iota_\Pi = \{\kappa : \Pi(\iota) > \Pi(\kappa)\}$ the set of players preceding player ι in the order Π for each player ι. Under these circumstances, the player ι's Shapley value in the coalitional game v is

$$\phi_\iota^{Shapley}(v) = \frac{1}{3!}\sum_{\Pi \in \Pi}[v(\perp_\Pi^\iota \cup \iota) - v(\perp_\Pi^\iota)] \qquad (A1.24)$$

As in Shubik (1962), I can give the characteristic function for the above coalitional game in an explicit way:

$$v(\{\varnothing\}) = 0$$

$$v(\{g\}) = \max_{\tau_l,\tau_c,n^*_{cK},r^l_d,r^c_d} N^1 W^1(\overline{V}) + N^2 W^2(\overline{V}^2) + B(A_c(n^*_{cK} - \chi)^\alpha \Xi^{1-\alpha}) +$$

$$\rho\left\{\begin{array}{l} \dfrac{p_l - \tau_l}{p_c + \tau_c} p_{al}\{N^1[F(t,h^1) - c^1_a] - N^2 c^2_a\} + A_c(n^*_{cK} - \chi)^\alpha \\ (\Xi)^{1-\alpha} - (1 - \delta)\Gamma + \dfrac{p_l - \tau_l}{p_c + \tau_c}[A_l(\overline{K} - n^*_{cK} + \chi)^\beta - \\ (H^2 - \Xi)^{1-\beta} - N^1 c^1_l - N^2 c^2_l] \end{array}\right\}$$

$$v(\{m_c\}) = \max\{\sigma_c[(p_c + \tau_c)A_c(n^*_{cK})^\alpha(\Xi)^{1-\alpha} - r^c_d n^*_{cK} - w_d \Xi \\ - (p_c + \tau_c)(1 - \delta)\Gamma],0\}$$

$$v(\{m_l\}) = \max\{\sigma_l[(p_l - \tau_l)A_l(\overline{K} - n^*_{cK})^\beta(H^2 - \Xi)^{1-\beta} - r^l_d(\overline{K} - n^*_{cK}) \\ - w_d(H^2 - J)],0\}$$

$$v(m_c,m_l) = \max_\chi\left\{\begin{array}{l} \sigma_c(p_c + \tau_c)A_c(n^*_{cK} - \chi)^\alpha(\Xi)^{1-\alpha} - \sigma_c r^c_d(n^*_{cK} - \chi) \\ \qquad\qquad\qquad\qquad\qquad\qquad\qquad - \sigma_c w_d \Xi \\ - \sigma_c(p_c + \tau_c)(1 - \delta)\Gamma + \sigma_l(p_l - \tau_l)A_l(\overline{K} \\ - n^*_{cK} + \chi)^\beta(H^2 - \Xi)^{1-\beta} \\ - \sigma_l r^l_d(\overline{K} - n^*_{cK} + \chi) - \sigma_l w_d(H^2 - \Xi) \end{array}\right\}$$

$$v(\{g,m_c\}) = \max_{\tau_l,\tau_c,n^*_{cK},r^c_d} N^1 W^1(\overline{V}^1 + N^2 W^2(\overline{V}^2)$$

$$+ B(A_c(n^*_{cK})^\alpha \Xi^{1-\alpha}) +$$

$$\rho\left\{\begin{array}{l} \dfrac{p_l - \tau_l}{p_c + \tau_c}[p_{al}\{N^1[F(t,h^1) - c^1_a] - N^2 c^2_a\} + (A_l(\overline{K} - n^*_{cK})^\beta \\ (H^2 - \Xi)^{1-\beta} - N^1 c^1_l - N^2 c^2_l)] \\ + A_c(n^*_{cK})^\alpha(\Xi)^{1-\alpha} - (1 - \delta)\Gamma \end{array}\right\}$$

$$+ \sigma_c[(p_c + \tau_c)A_c(n^*_{cK})^\alpha(\Xi)^{1-\alpha} - r^c_d n^*_{cK} - w_d \Xi \\ - (p_c + \tau_c)(1 - \delta)\Gamma]$$

$$v(\{g,m_l\}) = \underset{\tau_l,\tau_c,n^*_{cK},r^l_d}{\text{Max}} N^1 W^1(\overline{V}^1 + N^2 W^2(\overline{V}^2)$$

$$+ B(A_c(n^*_{cK})^\alpha \Xi^{1-\alpha}) +$$

$$\rho \left\{ \begin{array}{l} \dfrac{p_l - \tau_l}{p_c + \tau_c}[p_{al}\{N^1[F(t,h^1) - c^1_a] - N^2 c^2_a\} \\ + (A_l(\overline{K} - n^*_{cK})^\beta(H^2 - \Xi)^{1-\beta} - N^1 c^1_l - N^2 c^2_l)] \end{array} \right\}$$

$$+ A_c(n^*_{cK})^\alpha(\Xi)^{1-\alpha} - (1-\delta)\Gamma$$
$$+ \sigma_l[(p_l - \tau_l)A_l(\overline{K} - n^*_{cK})^\beta(H^2 - \Xi)^{1-\beta} - r^l_d(\overline{K} - n^*_{cK})$$
$$- w_d(H^2 - \Xi)]$$

$$v(\{g,m_c,m_l\}) = \underset{\tau_l,\tau_c,n^*_{cK},r^l_d,r^c_d,\chi}{\text{Max}} N^1 W^1(\overline{V}^1) + N^2 W^2(\overline{V}^2) +$$

$$B(A_c(n^*_{cK} - \chi)^\alpha \Xi^{1-\alpha}) +$$

$$\rho \left\{ \begin{array}{l} \dfrac{p_l - \tau_l}{p_c + \tau_c}p_{al}\{N^1[F(t,h^1) - c^1_a] - N^2 c^2_a\} + \\ \dfrac{p_l - \tau_l}{p_c + \tau_c}[A_l(\overline{K} - n^*_{cK} + \chi)^\beta(H^2 - \Xi)^{1-\beta} - N^1 c^1_l - N^2 c^2_l] \\ + A_c(n^*_{cK} - \chi)^\alpha(\Xi)^{1-\alpha} - (1-\delta)\Gamma \end{array} \right\}$$

$$+ \sigma_l[(p_l - \tau_l)A_l(\overline{K} - n^*_{cK} + \chi)^\beta(H^2 - \Xi)^{1-\beta} - r^l_d(\overline{K} - n^*_{cK} + \chi)$$
$$- w_d(H^2 - \Xi)]$$
$$+ \sigma_c[(p_c + \tau_c)A_c(n^*_{cK} - \chi)^\alpha(\Xi)^{1-\alpha} - r^c_d(n^*_{cK} - \chi) - w_d\Xi$$
$$- (p_c + \tau_c)(1-\delta)\Gamma]$$

Now I can solve the SPE by means of a backward solution as follows.

- Facing the given output prices $(p_c + \tau_c, p_l - \tau_l)$, the given factor prices (w_d, r^c_d, r^l_d) and the resulting allocations of factors $n^*_{ji}(i = L,K)$ to firm j, manager m_c decides χ to maximise $v(m_c,m_l)$, which implies that we have the following first order consition:[30]

$$- \sigma_c[(p_c + \tau_c)A_c\alpha(n^*_{cK} - \chi)^{\alpha-1}(\Xi)^{1-\alpha} - r^c_d]$$
$$+ \sigma_l[(p_l - \tau_l)A_l\beta(\overline{K} - n^*_{cK} + \chi)^{\beta-1}(H^2 - \Xi)^{1-\beta} - r^l_d] = 0$$

$$(A1.25)$$

---

[30] There is an implicit assumption, which is $\sigma_j \neq 0$, $\forall\ j = l,c$, in (A1.25).

- The government chooses the distorted relative output prices $(p_c + \tau_c, p_l - \tau_l)$, the interest rate affecting capital-intensive and labour-intensive firms (r_d^c, r_d^l), the resulting allocations of factors $n_{ji}^*(i = L, K)$ to firm $j = l, c$ to maximise $v(\{g, m_c, m_l\})$, subject to the treasury's budget constraint, which can be expressed by

$$(1 - \sigma_l)[(p_l - \tau_l)A_l(\overline{K} - n_{cK}^* + \chi)^\beta (H^2 - \Xi)^{1-\beta} - r_d^l(\overline{K} - n_{cK}^* + \chi)$$
$$- w_d(H^2 - \Xi)]$$

$$+ (1 - \sigma_c)[(p_c + \tau_c)A_c(n_{cK}^* - \chi)^\alpha (\Xi)^{1-\alpha} - r_d^c(n_{cK}^* - \chi) - w_d\Xi$$
$$- (p_c + \tau_c)(1 - \delta)\Gamma]$$

$$+ \phi_l \tau_l A_l(\overline{K} - n_{cK}^* + \chi)^\beta (H^2 - \Xi)^{1-\beta} \geq \tau_c A_c(n_{cK}^* - \chi)^\alpha (\Xi)^{1-\alpha} \tag{A1.26}$$

It is obvious that the equilibrium interest rate r_d^{*jm} under manager control in firm j equals $v_j r^*$ – that is, we have $r_d^{*jm} = v_j r^*$. Moreover, the government's decision should satisfy the following first-order conditions:

$$\frac{\rho}{p_c + \tau_c} \left\{ \begin{array}{l} p_{al}\{N^1[F(t, h^1) - c_a^1] - N^2 c_a^2\} + \\ [A_l(\overline{K} - n_{cK}^* + \chi)^\beta (H^2 - \Xi)^{1-\beta} - N^1 c_l^1 - N^2 c_l^2] \\ + \sigma_l A_l(\overline{K} - n_{cK}^* + \chi)^\beta (H^2 - \Xi)^{1-\beta} \end{array} \right\} \tag{A1.27}$$

$$- \vartheta^m \left\{ \begin{array}{l} \phi_l A_l(\overline{K} - n_{cK}^* + \chi)^\beta (H^2 - \Xi)^{1-\beta} - \\ (1 - \sigma_l)[-A_l(\overline{K} - n_{cK}^* + \chi)^\beta (H^2 - \Xi)^{1-\beta}] \end{array} \right\} = 0$$

$$- \rho \frac{p_l - \tau_l}{(p_c + \tau_c)^2} \left\{ \begin{array}{l} p_{al}\{N^1[F(t, h^1) - c_a^1] - N^2 c_a^2\} + \\ [A_l(\overline{K} - n_{cK}^* + \chi)^\beta (H^2 - \Xi)^{1-\beta} - N^1 c_l^1 - N^2 c_l^2] \end{array} \right\}$$

$$+ \sigma_c[A_c(n_{cK}^* - \chi)^\alpha (\Xi)^{1-\alpha} - (1 - \delta)\Gamma] \tag{A1.28}$$

$$\vartheta^m \{(1 - \sigma_c)[A_c(n_{cK}^* - \chi)^\alpha (\Xi)^{1-\alpha} - (1 - \delta)\Gamma]$$
$$- A_c(n_{cK}^* - \chi)^\alpha (\Xi)^{1-\alpha}\} = 0$$

$$B'(A_c(n_{cK}^* - \chi)^\alpha \Xi^{1-\alpha})A_c\alpha(n_{cK}^* - \chi)^{\alpha-1}\Xi^{1-\alpha} +$$

$$\rho\left\{ \begin{array}{c} -\dfrac{p_l - \tau_l}{p_c + \tau_c}A_l\beta(\overline{K} - n_{cK}^* + \chi)^{\beta-1}(H^2 - \Xi)^{1-\beta} \\ + A_c\alpha(n_{cK}^* - \chi)^{\alpha-1}(\Xi)^{1-\alpha} \end{array} \right\}$$

$$+ \sigma_l[-(p_l - \tau_l)A_l\beta(\overline{K} - n_{cK}^* + \chi)^{\beta-1}(H^2 - \Xi)^{1-\beta} + v_l r^*]$$
$$+ \sigma_c[(p_c + \tau_c)A_c\alpha(n_{cK}^* - \chi)^{\alpha-1}(\Xi)^{1-\alpha} - v_c r^*] \quad \text{(A1.29)}$$

$$\vartheta^m\left\{ \begin{array}{c} -\phi_l\tau_l A_l\beta(\overline{K} - n_{cK}^* + \chi)^{\beta-1}(H^2 - \Xi)^{1-\beta} + \\ (1-\sigma_l)[-(p_l - \tau_l)A_l\beta(\overline{K} - n_{cK}^* + \chi)^{\beta-1}(H^2 - \Xi)^{1-\beta} + v_l r^*] \\ + (1 - \sigma_c)[(p_c + \tau_c)A_c\alpha(n_{cK}^* - \chi)^{\alpha-1}(\Xi)^{1-\alpha} - v_c r^*] \\ - \tau_c A_c\alpha(n_{cK}^* - \chi)^{\alpha-1}(\Xi)^{1-\alpha} \end{array} \right\} = 0$$

where ϑ^m is the Lagrange multiplier under manager control for the treasury's budget constraint.

In sub-game perfect equilibrium under manager control, the equilibrium amount of capital used in the capital-intensive firm, denoted by $\tilde{n}_{cK}^{*m}$, must equal the resulting allocations of capital to this firm, denoted by n_{cK}^{*m} – that is, $\tilde{n}_{cK}^{*m} = n_{cK}^{*m}$. Thus, in sub-game perfect equilibrium, the amount of capital diverted outside from the capital-intensive firm to the labour-intensive firm should equal zero – that is, $\chi^* = 0$.

Plugging $\chi^* = 0$ into equations (A1.26), (A1.27), (A1.28) and (A1.29), I can solve the equilibrium tax rate in the labour-intensive firm τ_l^{*m}, the equilibrium subsidy rate in the capital-intensive firm τ_c^{*m} and the resulting allocations of capital n_{jK}^{*m} in firm $j = l,c$, which are equal to the equilibrium amount of factors used in that firm $\tilde{n}_{ji}^{*m}$ under manager control.

The equilibrium tax rate in the rural sector τ_a^{*m} and the equilibrium (nominal) urban wage w_d^{*m} under manager control are determined by

$$\tau_a^{*m} = p_a - p_{al}(p_l - \tau_l^{*m})$$

$$w_d^{*m} = w_l(p_l - \tau_l^{*m})$$

The other equilibrium endogenous variables under manager control – for example, the equilibrium surplus of the rural good per rural worker S^{*m}, the equilibrium investment I^{*m}, the equilibrium output of capital-intensive product q_c^{*m} and the equilibrium output of labour-intensive product q_l^{*m} under manager control – can be determined after τ_a^{*m}, τ_l^{*m}, τ_c^{*m}, $\tilde{n}_{ji}^{*m}$, w_d^{*m} and r_d^{*jm} have been solved.

Finally, based on the characteristic function for the above coalitional game, applying the Shapley value in (A1.24), we obtain

$$\phi_{m_c}^{\text{Shapley}} = \frac{1}{3!}\left\{2v(\{g\}) + [v(\{g, m_c\}) - v(\{m_c\})] + \right.$$
$$\left. [v(\{g,m_l\}) - v(\{m_l\})] + 2[v(\{g,m_c,m_l\}) - v(\{m_c,m_l\})]\right\}$$

$$\phi_{m_c}^{\text{Shapley}} = \frac{1}{3!}\left\{2v(\{m_c\}) + [v(\{g,m_c\}) - v(\{g\})] + \right.$$
$$\left. [v(\{m_c,m_l\}) - v(\{m_l\})] + 2[v(\{g,m_c,m_l\}) - v(\{g,m_l\})]\right\}$$

$$\phi_{m_l}^{\text{Shapley}} = \frac{1}{3!}\left\{2v(\{m_l\}) + [v(\{g,m_l\}) - v(\{g\})] + \right.$$
$$\left. [v(\{m_c,m_l\}) - v(\{m_c\})] + 2[v(\{g,m_c,m_l\}) - v(\{g,m_c\})]\right\}$$

Comparing equilibrium under manager control with that under government control yields the following proposition.

Proposition 6 To implement a catch-up type of CAD strategy in its country successfully, the developing country government always prefers its control over the exact use of the resulting allocation of capital to the firm $j = l,c$, denoted by n_{jK}^*, rather than that of manager m_j – that is, the government would like to deprive the firm of autonomy.[31]

Finally, from the proof of proposition 6 attached at the end of the appendix as a technical note, we know that, from the government's point of view, the root of equilibrium under manager control is inferior to that under government control when the manager has the arbitrage opportunity of diverting capital from one firm to the other, as described in first-order conditions in (A1.25). Had arbitrage opportunities for diverting capital from one firm to the other disappeared, equilibrium under manager control would be identical to that under government control for the developing country government. These arbitrage opportunities will not exist if either $\sigma_l = 0$ or $\sigma_c = 0$ – that is, either firm c or firm l is purely state-owned and has no ownership of cash flow. Therefore, we have the following corollary.

Corollary 1 Equilibrium with non-clearing markets under manager control depends on the exact value of σ_j – that is, on the ownership of a firm's cash flow. Moreover, the government prefers the exact value of σ_j to be zero under manager control – that is, the government prefers the firms to be owned completely by the state.[32]

---

[31] The justification for the developing country government's deprivation of a firm's autonomy is analogous to the case in Burkart, Panunzi and Shleifer (2003), which examines whether entrepreneurs want to surrender control of their firms, by comparing the potential benefits of owner control with the forgone benefits of rendering control to capable outside professional managers – although the role of capable outside professional managers is ignored in our model for tractability.

[32] It is assumed in the model that there is an information asymmetry between the government and the manager. Therefore, once the firm is state-owned and the cash flow is completely controlled by the government, there is no need for the government to deprive the manager of control rights over the use of capital and other resources. In reality, however, information between the government and manager is asymmetrical and the manager has some control in the use of cash flow. If the manager has the control right over the use of resources, the diversion of resources for the manager's on-the-job consumption and other moral hazard behaviour could occur. Therefore, the government would deprive the manager of autonomy, even if the firm was state-owned. In effect, this is what happened in the planning system in China, the Soviet Union and other socialist countries.

A1.4 Concluding remarks

There exist widespread distorted institutional arrangements and interventionist policies, such as price distortion, financial repression, trade restriction, the rationing of capital and foreign exchange, the licensing of investments, administrative monopoly and state owner-ship, in many developing countries, whether they are socialist or pre-viously socialist countries such as China, the former Soviet Union and eastern European countries, or non-socialist countries such as India and many Latin American countries. The main purpose of this appendix has been to construct a simple three-sector model to show that the fundamental logic of these distorted institutional arrange-ments and interventionist policies in a developing country arises from its government's attempt to develop advanced, capital-intensive industries when the characteristic of the country's endowments is rel-atively capital scarce due to its political leaders' aspiration for nation building, modernisation and political independence in the country.

Retrospectively, the CAD strategy seems to be extremely inappro-priate, and even absurd, according to today's thinking. It was initiated by idealistic nationalist leaders behaving as benevolent guardians with bounded rationality. Deeply influenced by their own aspirations for nation building, the prevailing view of economic development and Keynesian theory at that time, as well as the successful experi-ence of the Soviet Union's industrialisation under Stalin's leadership before the Second World War, most developing countries – socialist and non-socialist – adopted a catch-up type of CAD strategy to accel-erate the growth of capital-intensive, advanced sectors in their coun-tries following the Second World War. Many firms in the priority sectors of this strategy were non-viable in open, competitive markets because the priority sectors were not compatible with their economies' comparative advantages. The model shows that the gov-ernment intervention – including distorted prices for products and essential factors of production, highly centralised, planned resource allocation systems and a micro-management mechanism in which firms were deprived of autonomy – was endogenous to the needs of maximising resource mobilisation to build up the priority sectors and to support non-viable firms in those sectors. Thus, given the government's motivation – that is, pursuing a catch-up type of CAD strategy – these distorted economic institutions and interventionist policies in the developing countries were second-best arrangements.[33] Therefore, as Lin and Li (2008) show, unless the issue of firms' viability was addressed and the catch-up type of CAD strategy was abandoned, the implementation of price liberalisation, privatisation and the elimination of other distortions – as advocated by the Washington Consensus – resulted in poorer economic performance in developing countries than that achieved prior to the reforms.

Technical note

Proof of proposition 6   Proof by contradiction: it is obvious that equilibrium under manager control can be obtained by government control.[34] Thus, equilibrium under government control weakly dominates equilibrium under manager control from the viewpoint of the developing country government. If I can prove that equilibrium under manager control could not always equal equilibrium under government control, the developing country government will prefer equilibrium under government control to that under manager control, which is the result in proposition 6 – that is, developing country governments would like to deprive firms of autonomy.

Let us first assume that equilibrium under government control is always identical to that under manager control – that is, we have $\tau_c^{*m} = \tau_c^{*g}$, $\tau_l^{*m} = \tau_l^{*g}$ and $\tilde{n}_{ji}^{*m} = \tilde{n}_{ji}^{*g}$, etc.

---

[33] I share the view of Krueger (1995), that many of the policies that eventually became so inimical to growth appear to have been adopted for idealistic motives, and not for the narrow self-interest of the groups in the ruling coalition.

[34] The model set-up in this technical note could guarantee that either equilibrium under government control or equilibrium under manager control is unique.

From the first-order condition in (A1.21), I know that equilibrium under government control should satisfy

$$\frac{\rho}{p_c + \tau_c^{*g}} p_{al} \{ N^1[F(t,h^1) - c_a^1] - N^2 c_a^2 \} +$$

$$\frac{\rho}{p_c + \tau_c^{*g}} (A_l(\overline{K} - \tilde{n}_{cK}^{*g})^\beta (H^2 - \Xi)^{1-\beta} - N^1 c_l^1 - N^2 c_l^2) - \quad (A1.30)$$

$$\hbar^g \phi_l A_l (\overline{K} - \tilde{n}_{cK}^{*g})^\beta (H^2 - \Xi)^{1-\beta} + \chi_l^g \sigma_l A_l (\overline{K} - \tilde{n}_{cK}^{*g})^\beta$$
$$(H^2 - \Xi)^{1-\beta} = 0$$

Substituting $\chi^* = 0$ into (A1.27) implies that, in SPE under manager control, we have

$$\frac{\rho}{p_c + \tau_c^{*m}} \begin{cases} p_{al} \{ N^1[F(t,h^1) - c_a^1] - N^2 c_a^2 \} + \\ [A_l(\overline{K} - \tilde{n}_{cK}^{*m})^\beta (H^2 - \Xi)^{1-\beta} - N^1 c_l^1 - N^2 c_l^2] \end{cases}$$

$$+ \sigma_l A_l (\overline{K} - \tilde{n}_{cK}^{*m})^\beta (H^2 - \Xi)^{1-\beta} \quad (A1.31)$$

$$- \vartheta^m \begin{cases} \phi_l A_l (\overline{K} - \tilde{n}_{cK}^{*m})^\beta (H^2 - \Xi)^{1-\beta} + \\ (1 - \sigma_l)[A_l(\overline{K} - \tilde{n}_{cK}^{*m})^\beta (H^2 - \Xi)^{1-\beta}] \end{cases} = 0$$

Comparing (A1.30) with (A1.31), under the assumption that equilibrium under government control is identical to that under manager control, we must have $\hbar^g = \vartheta^m$ and $\chi_l^g \sigma_l = -\vartheta^m(1 - \sigma_l) + \sigma_l$.

The first-order condition in (A1.22) implies that, equilibrium under government control should satisfy

$$- \rho \frac{p_l - \tau_l^{*g}}{(p_c + \tau_c^{*g})^2} p_{al} \{ N^1[F(t,h^1) - c_a^1] - N^2 c_a^2 \} +$$

$$- \rho \frac{p_l - \tau_l^{*g}}{(p_c + \tau_c^{*g})^2} (A_l(\overline{K} - \tilde{n}_{cK}^{*g})^\beta (H^2 - \Xi)^{1-\beta} - N^1 c_l^1 - N^2 c_l^2) \quad (A1.32)$$

$$- \hbar^g A_c(\tilde{n}_{cK}^{*g})^\alpha \Xi^{1-\alpha} + \chi_c^g \sigma_c [A_c(\tilde{n}_{cK}^{*g})^\alpha (\Xi)^{1-\alpha} - (1 - \delta)\Gamma] = 0$$

Replacing $\chi^* = 0$ in SPE under manager control with (A1.28) yields

$$-\rho\frac{p_l - \tau_l^{*m}}{(p_c + \tau_c^{*m})^2}\left\{\begin{array}{l} p_{al}\{N^1[F(t,h^1) - c_a^1] - N^2c_a^2\} + \\ [A_l(\overline{K} - \tilde{n}_{cK}^{*m})^\beta(H^2 - \Xi)^{1-\beta} - N^1c_l^1 - N^2c_l^2] \end{array}\right\}$$

$$+ \sigma_c[A_c(\tilde{n}_{cK}^{*m})^\alpha(\Xi)^{1-\alpha} - (1-\delta)\Gamma] \qquad \text{(A1.33)}$$

$$\vartheta^m\{(1-\sigma_c)[A_c(\tilde{n}_{cK}^{*m})^\alpha(\Xi)^{1-\alpha} - (1-\delta)\Gamma] - A_c(\tilde{n}_{cK}^{*m})^\alpha$$
$$(\Xi)^{1-\alpha}\} = 0$$

Comparing (A1.32) with (A1.33) implies that, under the assumption that equilibrium under government control is identical to that under manager control, we must have $\chi^g = \vartheta^m$ and $\chi^g\sigma_c = \sigma_c + \vartheta^m(1-\sigma_c)$.

Replacing r_d^{*jg} with $v_j r^*$ in (A1.23) means that, under government control, we have

$$B'(A_c(\tilde{n}_{cK}^{*g})^\alpha\Xi^{1-\alpha})A_c\alpha(\tilde{n}_{cK}^{*g})^{\alpha-1}\Xi^{1-\alpha} +$$

$$-\rho\frac{p_l - \tau_l^{*g}}{p_c + \tau_c^{*g}}A_l\beta(\overline{K} - \tilde{n}_{cK}^{*g})^{\beta-1}(H^2 - \Xi)^{1-\beta} + \rho A_c\alpha(\tilde{n}_{cK}^{*g})^{\alpha-1}\Xi^{1-\alpha}$$

$$+ \hbar^g[-\phi_l\tau_l^{*g}A_l\beta(\overline{K} - \tilde{n}_{cK}^{*g})^{\beta-1}(H^2 - \Xi)^{1-\beta} - \tau_c^{*g}A_c\alpha(\tilde{n}_{cK}^{*g})^{\alpha-1}\Xi^{1-\alpha}]$$

$$+ \chi^g\sigma_c[(p_c + \tau_c^{*g})A_c\alpha(\tilde{n}_{cK}^{*g})^{\alpha-1}(\Xi)^{1-\alpha} - v_cr^*] \qquad \text{(A1.34)}$$

$$+ \chi^g\sigma_l[-(p_l - \tau_l^{*g})A_l\beta(\overline{K} - \tilde{n}_{cK}^{*g})^{\beta-1}(H^2 - \Xi)^{1-\beta} + v_lr^*] = 0$$

Substituting $r_d^{*jm} = v_jr^*$ and $\chi^* = 0$ into (A1.25) implies that the SPE under manager control should satisfy

$$\sigma_c[(p_c + \tau_c^{*m})A_c\alpha(\tilde{n}_{cK}^{*m})^{\alpha-1}(\Xi)^{1-\alpha} - v_cr^*] =$$
$$\sigma_l[(p_l - \tau_l^{*m})A_l\beta(\overline{K} - \tilde{n}_{cK}^{*m})^{\beta-1}(H^2 - \Xi)^{1-\beta} - v_lr^*] \qquad \text{(A1.35)}$$

Plugging (A1.35) and $\chi^* = 0$ into (A1.29) delivers

$$B'(A_c(\tilde{n}_{cK}^*)^\alpha\Xi^{1-\alpha})A_c\alpha(\tilde{n}_{cK}^*)^{\alpha-1}\Xi^{1-\alpha}$$

$$+ \rho\left\{\begin{array}{l} -\dfrac{p_l - \tau_l^{*m}}{p_c + \tau_c^{*m}}A_l\beta(\overline{K} - \tilde{n}_{cK}^*)^{\beta-1}(H^2 - \Xi)^{1-\beta} \\ \\ \quad\quad + A_c\alpha(\tilde{n}_{cK}^*)^{\alpha-1}(\Xi)^{1-\alpha} \end{array}\right\} \text{(A1.36)}$$

$$\vartheta^m \left\{ \begin{array}{c} - \phi_l \tau_l^{*m} A_l \beta (\overline{K} - \tilde{n}_{cK}^*)^{\beta-1} (H^2 - \Xi)^{1-\beta} - \tau_c^{*m} A_c \alpha (\tilde{n}_{cK}^*)^{\alpha-1} \\ (\Xi)^{1-\alpha} \\ + [-(p_l - \tau_l^{*m}) A_l \beta (\overline{K} - \tilde{n}_{cK}^*)^{\beta-1} (H^2 - \Xi)^{1-\beta} + v_l r^*] \\ + [(p_c + \tau_c^{*m}) A_c \alpha (\tilde{n}_{cK}^*)^{\alpha-1} (\Xi)^{1-\alpha} - v_c r^*] \end{array} \right\} = 0$$

Comparison of (A1.34) with (A1.36) implies that, under the assumption that equilibrium under government control is identical to that under manager control, we must have $\hbar^g = \vartheta^m$, $\lambda_c^g \sigma_c = \vartheta^m$ and $\lambda_l^g \sigma_l = \vartheta^m$.

Substituting $\lambda_c^g \sigma_c = \vartheta^m$ into $\lambda_c^g \sigma_c = \sigma_c + \vartheta^m (1 - \sigma_c)$ gives $\vartheta^m = 1$. Combining $\lambda_l^g \sigma_l = -\vartheta^m (1 - \sigma_l) + \sigma_l$ and $\lambda_l^g \sigma_l = \vartheta^m$ yields $\sigma_l / (2 - \sigma_l) = \vartheta^m$, which means that $\sigma_l = 1$, owing to $\vartheta^m = 1$. Furthermore, we have $\lambda_l^g \equiv 1$, $\hbar^g \equiv 1$ and $\lambda_c^g \equiv 1 / \sigma_c$ after a simple arithmetic operation.

It is well known that the Lagrange multiplier has an economic interpretation as the shadow price associated with the constraint. The necessary conditions above guarantee that equilibrium under government control is always identical to that under manager control – that is, $\vartheta^m = 1$, $\sigma_l = 1$, $\lambda_l^g \equiv 1$, $\hbar^g \equiv 1$ and $\lambda_c^g \equiv 1 / \sigma_c$; this implies that equilibrium under government control that is identical to that under manager control is a special case only.

Therefore, developing country governments prefer equilibrium under government control to that of manager control.

QED.

Data description

122 countries

Country	TCI (1963–99)		Growth rate of GDP per capita (%) (1962–99)		Black market premium (1960–99)		Number of procedures (1999)		IEF (1970–2005)		Expropriation risk (1982–97)		Executive de facto independence (1945–98)		Openness (1960~2003)	
	Mean	S.D.	Mean	S.D.	Mean	S.D.	Mean	S.D.	Mean	S.D.	Mean	S.D.	Mean	S.D.	Mean	S.D.
Albania	1.771	0.095	1.713	9.190	7.503	6.492			5.483	0.742	7.264				48.321	15.940
Algeria	2.157	0.979	1.377	8.127	147.937	137.826			4.363	0.481	6.763				56.805	15.229
Argentina	2.564	0.588	0.915	5.742	40.934	77.874	14.000		5.365	1.172	6.313		3.140		16.423	6.248
Australia	1.073	0.162	2.150	2.036	0.000	0.000	2.000		7.585	0.461	9.379		7.000		32.905	5.337
Austria	1.083	0.071	2.790	1.831	0.000	0.000	9.000		7.149	0.545	9.743		7.000		69.527	15.824
Bahamas	1.929	0.845	1.504	6.985	12.539	12.764					7.793				129.182	10.750
Bangladesh	4.302	0.902	1.192	4.091	96.876	66.359			4.990	0.969	5.413				22.414	5.646

Barbados	1.283	0.521	2.449	4.566	7.442	4.861	8.000	5.615	0.142		7.000	118.786	14.759
Belgium	1.017	0.122	2.626	1.959	0.000	0.000		7.316	0.179	9.686		120.602	25.441
Belize	1.067	0.072	3.256	4.168	26.857	21.769		6.235	0.497			116.954	9.390
Benin	13.694	2.026	0.861	3.185	3.424	4.533		5.212	0.406			40.868	12.273
Bhutan	4.514		4.247	3.278	3.045	3.521						68.883	10.109
Bolivia	7.341	2.905	0.377	3.590	32.334	84.457	20.000	5.915	1.095	5.600	3.520	49.479	4.896
Botswana	1.791	0.801	6.421	5.132	13.180	11.245		6.578	0.681	8.007		103.668	24.533
Brazil	5.373	1.195	2.371	4.076	29.063	36.841	15.000	5.207	0.868	7.881	3.692	17.317	4.359
Bulgaria	1.372	0.089	1.541	5.288	7.423	10.158	10.000	5.536	0.889	9.036	3.679	90.813	16.009
Cameroon	7.018	1.626	0.977	5.993	3.431	4.531		5.597	0.144	6.463		48.559	9.062
Canada	1.531	0.199	2.110	2.097	0.000	0.000	2.000	7.858	0.282	9.721	7.000	55.645	14.057
Central African Republic	9.830	2.221	-0.837	3.924	3.271	4.456						53.552	13.560
Chile	4.307	1.223	2.595	4.798	38.157	104.680	10.000	6.554	1.345	7.800	3.667	46.041	14.844
China	4.165	1.327	6.003	7.381	71.004	111.533	12.000	5.397	0.525	8.114	2.321	26.614	16.924
Colombia	4.466	0.701	1.780	2.117	7.993	7.510	18.000	5.282	0.256	7.350	5.074	30.873	5.286
Congo	6.847	2.614	1.190	5.896	2.866	4.064				5.146		104.950	19.420
Costa Rica	2.190	0.683	1.833	3.350	40.799	67.249		6.730	0.755	7.038		70.816	13.687
Croatia	1.581	0.637	0.884	8.096	37.525	25.826	12.000	5.855	0.680		3.192	102.438	19.668
Cyprus	1.308	0.310	5.357	4.515	4.671	4.550		6.327	0.680	8.486		104.364	8.351
Denmark	1.178	0.079	2.100	2.230	0.000	0.000	3.000	7.268	0.502	9.721	7.000	64.511	7.827
Dominican Republic	2.532	0.368	2.800	5.232	31.641	36.064	21.000			6.356	3.340	59.607	20.106

122 countries

Country	TCI (1963–99)		Growth rate of GDP per capita (%) (1962–99)		Black market premium (1960–99)		Number of procedures (1999)		IEF (1970–2005)		Expropriation risk (1982–97)		Executive de facto independence (1945–98)		Openness (1960~2003)	
	Mean	S.D.	Mean	S.D.	Mean	S.D.	Mean	S.D.	Mean	S.D.	Mean	S.D.	Mean	S.D.	Mean	S.D.
Ecuador	3.878	1.238	1.263	3.381	20.225	24.613	16.000		5.300	0.592	6.763		4.148		50.157	9.744
Egypt	2.012	0.238	3.013	2.913	39.256	45.442	11.000				6.800		3.519		48.161	13.088
El Salvador	4.229	1.569	0.825	3.925	42.640	48.101			6.468	1.264	5.206				56.661	9.927
Ethiopia	17.921	2.621	0.326	7.127	72.262	73.517					6.047				32.004	10.522
Fiji	1.564	0.214	1.711	4.700	1.605	1.939			5.963	0.231					101.288	15.192
Finland	1.237	0.116	2.885	3.009	0.000	0.000	5.000		7.371	0.462	9.721		7.000		54.250	10.204
France	1.106	0.096	2.519	1.664	0.000	0.000	15.000		6.645	0.432	9.707		5.283		38.959	9.083
Gabon	2.119	0.759	2.538	10.245	1.740	4.035			4.944	0.470	7.556				93.218	15.593
Gambia	5.442	3.157	0.595	3.398	6.511	11.907					8.385				101.192	17.250
Ghana	5.962	2.075	0.071	4.253	248.144	729.713	10.000		5.159	1.390	6.219		1.943		47.462	25.698
Greece	1.337	0.087	3.200	3.878	5.412	5.028	15.000		6.394	0.532	7.481		5.792		40.066	10.166
Guatemala	3.303	0.279	1.230	2.500	12.346	15.467			6.321	0.542	5.156				39.266	7.322
Guyana	0.733		0.935	5.216	209.506	270.332			6.242	0.556	5.956				151.372	49.475
Honduras	3.183	0.790	0.820	2.946	12.008	26.842			6.180	0.359	5.413				68.718	16.915
Hong Kong	0.713	0.071	5.192	4.445	-0.416	1.383					8.488				209.386	52.589
Hungary	1.151	0.183	3.338	4.210	165.435	155.711	8.000		6.489	1.059	9.079		3.735		86.700	25.216
Iceland	0.802	0.134	2.823	3.809	1.233	1.423			6.906	1.102	9.700				72.982	6.502

India	3.635	0.421	2.573	3.077	26.530	24.692	10.000	5.744	0.729	8.069	6.959	15.517	6.343
Indonesia	3.073	0.408	3.581	3.974	273.451	806.400	11.000	5.863	0.535	7.475	2.981	44.716	16.991
Iran			0.231	7.115	464.833	857.111				4.694		38.814	16.870
Iraq	1.646	0.577	-2.515	18.460	851.008	2093.052				2.400			
Ireland	1.853	0.507	4.179	2.806	0.600	3.795	3.000	7.491	0.642	9.721	7.000	105.765	31.741
Israel	1.287	0.232	2.744	3.677	14.077	17.706	5.000	5.686	1.283	8.513	7.000	79.064	23.283
Italy	1.292	0.134	2.794	2.143	0.000	0.000	16.000	6.422	0.656	9.457	7.000	40.020	8.718
Jamaica	3.248	0.621	0.756	4.339	19.076	17.070	6.000	6.200	1.023	7.044	7.000	87.759	15.792
Japan	1.680	0.083	4.056	3.678	1.750	3.350	11.000	7.071	0.316	9.721	7.000	20.925	3.495
Jordan	1.936	0.492	1.980	7.193	3.399	2.899	14.000	6.335	0.698	6.556	2.208	119.307	14.334
Kenya	0.335	0.030	1.241	4.785	15.722	14.031	11.000	5.973	0.786	6.406	3.250	60.309	7.232
Kuwait	1.090	0.477	-3.916	8.708	0.001	0.399		6.609	0.817	7.056		96.580	11.295
Latvia	1.638	0.010	2.893	7.074	7.233	6.266	7.000	6.622	0.818		3.333	104.600	20.540
Lesotho	8.719	2.037	3.935	6.891	9.133	8.125						112.698	33.884
Libya	0.836	0.176	3.425	16.053	82.000	127.559				5.088		77.574	18.966
Luxembourg	0.914	0.101	3.163	3.267	0.375	0.466		7.703	0.105	10.000		198.318	32.906
Macao	0.384	0.060	2.666	4.375								156.762	28.830
Madagascar	5.373	0.498	-1.041	4.032	15.000	21.331	17.000	5.316	0.599	4.686	3.684	40.325	9.212
Malawi	8.631	2.923	1.309	5.380	36.658	31.917	12.000	5.038	0.397	6.863	1.571	60.909	8.653
Malaysia	1.854	0.191	3.926	3.483	1.172	1.634	7.000	6.819	0.382	8.150	5.381	122.600	49.604
Malta	1.143	0.091	5.196	4.244	2.724	5.448		6.236	0.663	7.875		162.837	27.787
Mauritius	1.121	0.447	4.355	1.678	4.892	7.090		6.669	0.893			116.900	13.110
Mexico	2.969	0.242	1.982	3.395	4.772	8.816	15.000	6.159	0.591	7.469	3.241	31.384	16.422
Moldova	4.073	0.611	-1.986	10.241	0.000							122.079	25.610
Mongolia	3.697	0.860	-0.258	6.501	0.635	3.085	5.000			7.950	3.333	120.161	32.221

122 countries

Country	TCI (1963–99)		Growth rate of GDP per capita (%) (1962–99)		Black market premium (1960–99)		Number of procedures (1999)		IEF (1970–2005)		Expropriation risk (1982–97)		Executive de facto independence (1945–98)		Openness (1960~2003)	
	Mean	S.D.	Mean	S.D.	Mean	S.D.	Mean	S.D.	Mean	S.D.	Mean	S.D.	Mean	S.D.	Mean	S.D.
Morocco	3.201	0.383	1.926	4.544	7.673	6.987	13.000		5.600	0.526	6.713		1.930		51.277	10.001
Namibia	3.711		-0.226	2.509	1.230	2.130			6.239	0.351	5.400				114.971	16.921
Nepal	4.174	0.342	1.359	2.893	33.574	34.464			5.448	0.271					33.297	15.010
Netherlands	1.158	0.204	2.253	1.946	0.000	0.000	8.000		7.620	0.305	9.979		7.000		100.484	12.498
Netherlands Antilles	0.767	0.110	-1.846	1.312	-0.333	2.417										
New Zealand	1.061	0.188	1.420	2.906	0.600	3.795	3.000		7.656	0.900	9.736		7.000		57.134	6.072
Nigeria	9.338	6.549	0.801	7.314	86.273	109.203	9.000		4.659	0.915	5.300		2.784		49.170	24.309
Norway	0.914	0.072	3.090	1.723	0.000	0.000	4.000		6.890	0.534	9.850		7.000		73.425	3.821
Oman	1.036	0.151	6.296	16.124	0.460	1.061			7.125	0.440	7.321				93.117	12.928
Pakistan	6.114	1.221	2.564	2.397	38.871	42.583	8.000		5.190	0.632	6.150		4.083		32.965	4.991
Panama	2.738	0.550	2.186	4.133	0.000	0.000	7.000		6.811	0.590	6.063		3.611		154.750	27.245
Papua New Guinea	7.250	1.541	1.177	4.902	15.938	15.557					7.743				82.113	17.158
Paraguay	2.852	0.450	1.598	3.634	25.390	37.524			6.041	0.405	6.900		3.769		48.239	20.040
Peru	5.128	1.162	0.783	4.825	36.554	64.825	8.000		5.648	1.496	6.206				34.543	5.348
Philippines	4.571	1.143	1.304	3.004	9.418	13.474	14.000		6.176	0.725	5.788		4.038		56.720	24.885

Country													
Poland	1.704	0.327	3.320	3.604	351.565	270.847	11.000	5.755	1.103	7.814	3.538	51.814	5.736
Portugal	1.265	0.257	3.684	3.804	4.263	7.944	12.000	6.635	1.028	9.006	3.538	57.577	11.450
Puerto Rico	3.814	0.718	3.760	2.936								133.300	24.180
Qatar	1.595	0.387			0.203	0.259				7.857		80.400	6.756
Romania	1.086	0.046	0.400	5.217	169.469	158.714	16.000	5.149	0.711	7.557	3.180	60.521	11.528
Russia	0.999	0.108	-1.259	7.645	520.000	576.479	20.000			8.500	2.796	56.640	19.001
Saudi Arabia	1.675	1.101											
Senegal	8.914	2.469	0.003	4.200	3.431	4.531	16.000	5.506	0.494	5.925	3.000	62.380	14.527
Sierra Leone			-0.780	5.760	129.831	308.869	16.000	4.994	0.708	5.708		48.373	11.093
Singapore	1.406	0.203	5.576	4.289	0.800	0.988	7.000	8.364	0.365	9.394	3.421		
Slovak Republic	1.176	0.004											
Slovenia	1.071	0.112	2.123	4.236	10.000	6.880	9.000	5.811	0.453		3.808	118.000	12.035
South Africa	1.853	0.162	0.924	3.562	4.239	11.191	9.000	6.364	0.537	7.350	7.000	50.766	5.868
South Korea	2.816	0.493	5.797	3.615	15.251	24.015	13.000			8.569	3.140	53.775	18.238
Spain	1.267	0.199	3.332	2.698	2.344	2.235	11.000	6.750	0.508	9.550	3.471	35.180	12.544
Sri Lanka	2.728	0.341	2.831	1.983	50.615	50.224	8.000	5.720	0.407	6.538	6.176	70.775	10.682
Sudan	6.761	1.119		5.531	87.922	155.904				4.019		28.406	5.289
Suriname	2.409	0.532	0.217	6.114	14.683	8.356				5.169		94.879	29.815
Swaziland	3.817	0.733	2.008	4.193	11.283	7.128						146.657	30.193
Sweden	1.206	0.124	2.198	1.993	0.000	0.000	6.000	6.856	0.681	9.500	7.000	58.955	13.210
Switzerland	0.992	0.086	1.393	2.265	0.000	0.000	7.000	8.179	0.168	9.986	7.000	64.777	8.952
Syria	2.058	0.755	2.559	8.022	128.798	211.522	13.000			5.413		51.880	13.155
Tanzania	3.233	0.370	1.297	2.384	86.952	92.424		5.213	1.183	6.888	3.000	48.043	9.123
Thailand	7.201	2.613	4.641	3.640	0.418	2.889	9.000	6.514	0.386	7.644	3.039	60.693	28.782

122 countries

Country	TCI (1963–99)		Growth rate of GDP per capita (%) (1962–99)		Black market premium (1960–99)		Number of procedures (1999)	IEF (1970–2005)		Expropriation risk (1982–97)		Executive de facto independence (1945–98)		Openness (1960–2003)	
	Mean	S.D.	Mean	S.D.	Mean	S.D.	Mean	Mean	S.D.	Mean	S.D.	Mean	S.D.	Mean	S.D.
Togo	9.660	2.364	1.270	6.390	3.431	4.531		4.979	0.326	6.500				83.123	18.104
Trinidad and Tobago	1.475	0.446	2.043	4.713	30.029	20.051				7.294				89.984	18.725
Tunisia	2.891	1.243	3.117	3.613	27.354	41.695	9.000	5.613	0.557	6.506		1.625		69.147	22.894
Turkey	4.586	0.968	1.937	4.124	18.921	20.025	13.000	5.181	0.812	7.288		5.943		30.608	16.899
Uganda	6.236	0.376	2.259	3.224	198.418	301.088	11.000	5.332	1.640	4.800		2.735		35.186	9.543
United Arab Emirates	0.365	0.013	-3.028	8.110	-1.255	3.172				6.944				110.931	17.137
United Kingdom	1.358	0.154	2.149	1.795	0.000	0.000	5.000	7.626	0.766	9.764		7.000		49.873	6.861
United States	1.588	0.108	2.193	1.979	0.000	0.000	4.000	8.135	0.273	9.979		7.000		17.046	5.272
Uruguay	2.036	0.430	0.887	4.408	11.699	26.516	10.000	6.304	0.426	6.938		4.712		35.923	7.589
Venezuela	2.826	0.843			26.885	62.964	14.000	5.254	0.900	7.106		5.093			
Zambia	5.909	1.694	-0.776	4.695	85.435	119.817	6.000	5.653	1.336	6.669		2.257		77.325	13.388
Zimbabwe	5.118	1.358	0.450	5.847	52.239	56.792	5.000	3.912	0.855	6.025		4.643		53.964	16.555

Note: S.D. = standard deviation.

References

Abramovitz, M. (1995). 'The Elements of Social Capability'. In D. Perkins and B. H. Koo (eds.), *Social Capability and Long-term Economic Growth*. New York: St Martin's Press, 19–47.

Acemolgu, D. (2007a). 'Introduction to Economic Growth'. Mimeo. Department of Economics, Massachusetts Institute of Technology, Cambridge, MA.

(2007b). 'Modeling Inefficient Institutions'. In R. Blundell, W. K. Newey and T. Persson (eds.), *Advances in Economics and Econometrics, Theory and Applications: Ninth World Congress of the Econometric Society*. Cambridge: Cambridge University Press, 341–80.

Acemoglu, D., P. Aghion and F. Zilibotti (2006). 'Distance to Technology Frontier, Selection and Economic Growth'. *Journal of the European Economic Association*, 4 (1), 37–74.

Acemoglu, D., S. Johnson and J. A. Robinson (2001). 'The Colonial Origins of Comparative Development: An Empirical Investigation'. *American Economic Review*, 91 (5), 1369–401.

(2002). 'Reversal of Fortune: Geography and Institutions in the Making of the Modern World Income Distribution'. *Quarterly Journal of Economics*, 117 (4), 1231–94.

(2003). 'An African Success Story: Botswana'. In D. Rodrik (ed.), *In Search of Prosperity: Analytic Narratives on Economic Growth*. Princeton, NJ: Princeton University Press, 80–119.

(2005). 'Institutions as the Fundamental Cause of Long-run Growth'. In P. Aghion and S. N. Durlauf (eds.), *Handbook of Economic Growth*, vol. I, part A. Amsterdam: Elsevier Science, 385–472.

Akamatsu, K. (1962). 'A Historical Pattern of Economic Growth in Developing Countries'. *Developing Economies*, 1 (1), 3–25.

Allen, R. C. (2003). *Farm to Factory: A Reinterpretation of the Soviet Industrial Revolution*. Princeton, NJ: Princeton University Press.

Amsden, A. (1989). *Asia's Next Giant*. Oxford: Oxford University Press.

Aslund, A. (1991). 'Gorbachev, Perestroika, and Economic Crisis'. *Problems of Communism*, 40 (1–2), 18–41.

Bairoch, P. (1993). *Economics and World History: Myths and Paradoxes*. Chicago: University of Chicago Press.

Barro, R. J. (1998). *Determinants of Economic Growth: A Cross-country Empirical Study*. Cambridge, MA: MIT Press.

Bauer, P. T. (1984). *Reality and Rhetoric: Studies in the Economics of Development*. Cambridge, MA: Harvard University Press.

Baumol, W. (1994). 'Multivariate Growth Patterns: Contagion and Common Forces as Possible Sources of Convergence'. In W. Baumol, R. Nelson and E. Wolff (eds.), *Convergence of Productivity: Cross-national Studies and Historical Evidence*. New York: Oxford University Press, 62–85.

Bénassy, J.-P. (1977). 'On Quantity Signals and the Foundations of Effective Demand Theory'. *Scandinavian Journal of Economics*, 79 (2), 147–68.

 (2008). 'Non-clearing Markets in General Equilibrium'. In S. N. Durlauf and L. E. Blume (eds.), *New Palgrave Dictionary of Economics,* vol. VI (2nd edn.). London: Macmillan, 62–9.

Bernard, A. B., S. J. Redding and P. K. Schott (2007). 'Comparative Advantage and Heterogeneous Firms'. *Review of Economic Studies*, 74 (1), 31–66.

Bhagwati, J. (1984). 'Development Economics: What Have We Learned?'. *Asian Development Review*, 2 (1), 24–9.

Binswanger, H. P., and V. W. Ruttan (1978). *Induced Innovation: Technology, Institutions, and Development*. Baltimore: Johns Hopkins University Press.

Blanchard, O., R. Dornbusch, P. R. Krugman, R. Layard and L. Summers (1991). *Reform in Eastern Europe*. Cambridge, MA: MIT Press.

Blanchard, O., and L. Summers (1987). 'Hysteresis in Unemployment'. *European Economic Review*, 31 (1/2), 288–95.

Bockstette, V., A. Chanda and L. Putterman (2002). 'States and Markets: The Advantage of an Early Start'. *Journal of Economic Growth*, 7 (4), 347–69.

Boserup, E. (1965). *The Conditions of Agricultural Growth*. Chicago: Aldine.

Brada, J. C. (1996). 'Privatization Is Transition, or Is It?'. *Journal of Economic Perspectives*, 10 (2), 67–86.

Braudel, F. (1984). *Civilization and Capitalism, 15th–18th Century*, vol. III, *The Perspective of the World*. New York: Harper and Row.

Burkart, M., F. Panunzi and A. Shleifer (2003). 'Family Firms'. *Journal of Finance*, 58 (5), 2167–202.

Chanda, A., and L. Putterman (2007). 'Early Starts, Reversals and Catch-up in the Process of Economic Development'. *Scandinavian Journal of Economics*, 109 (2), 387–413.

Chang, H. J. (1994). *The Political Economy of Industrial Policy*. London: Macmillan.

Chang, H. J., and P. Noland (1995). 'Europe versus Asia: Contrasting Path to the Reform of Centrally Planned Systems of Political Economy'. In H. J. Chang and P. Nolan (eds.), *The Transformation of the Communist Economies*. London: Macmillan, 3–45.

Chenery, H. B. (1958). 'The Role of Industrialization in Development Programmes'. In A. N. Agarwala and S. P. Singh (eds.), *The Economics of Underdevelopment*. Mumbai: Oxford University Press, 450–71.

—— (1960). 'Patterns of Industrial Growth'. *American Economic Review*, 50 (4), 624–54.

—— (1961). 'Comparative Advantage and Development Policy'. *American Economic Review*, 51 (1), 18–51.

Cipolla, C. M. (1980). *Before the Industrial Revolution: European Society and Economy, 1000–1700* (2nd edn.). New York: W. W. Norton.

Clark, G. (2007). *A Farewell to Alms: A Brief Economic History of the World*. Princeton, NJ: Princeton University Press.

Clark, G., and R. C. Feenstra (2001). *Technology in the Great Divergence*, Working Paper no. 8596. National Bureau of Economic Research, Cambridge, MA.

CPC Central Committee, Documentation and Research Office (1955). *Documents of the Second Session of the First National People's Congress of the PRC* (in Chinese). Beijing: People's Press.

De Soto, H. (1987). *The Other Path*. New York: Harper & Row.

Deininger, K., and L. Squire (1996). 'A New Data Set Measuring Income Inequality'. *World Bank Economic Review*, 10 (3), 565–91.

Dewatripont, M., and E. Maskin (1995). 'Credit and Efficiency in Centralized and Decentralized Economies'. *Review of Economic Studies*, 62 (4), 541–56.

Dhar, P. N. (2003). *Evolution of Economic Policy in India: Selected Essays*. Oxford: Oxford University Press.

Diamond, J. M. (1997). *Guns, Germs, and Steel: The Fates of Human Societies*. New York: W. W. Norton.

Djankov, S., R. La Porta, F. Lopez-de-Silanes and A. Shleifer (2002). 'Regulation of Entry'. *Quarterly Journal of Economics*, 117 (1), 1–37.

Dollar, D. (1992). 'Outward-oriented Developing Economies Really Do Grow More Rapidly: Evidence from 95 Developing Countries, 1976–85'. *Economic Development and Cultural Change*, 40 (3), 523–44.

Dollar, D., and A. Kraay (2003). 'Institutions, Trade and Growth'. *Journal of Monetary Economics*, 50 (1), 133–62.

Dutt, A. K. (1992). 'The Origins of Uneven Development: The Indian Subcontinent'. *American Economic Review, Papers and Proceedings of the Hundred and Fourth Annual Meeting of the American Economic Association*, 82 (2), 146–50.

Dutt, R., and K. P. M. Sundharam (2006). *Indian Economy* (54th edn.). New Delhi: Chand.

Easterly, W. R. (2001a). 'The Lost Decades: Explaining Developing Countries' Stagnation in Spite of Policy Reform 1980–1998'. *Journal of Economic Growth*, 6 (2), 135–57.

—— (2001b). *The Elusive Quest for Growth: Economists' Adventures and Misadventures in the Tropics*. Cambridge, MA: MIT Press.

—— (2006). *The White Man's Burden: Why the West's Efforts to Aid the Rest Have Done So Much Ill and So Little Good*. New York: Penguin Books.

Easterly, W. R., and R. Levine (2003). 'Tropics, Germs, and Crops: How Endowments Influence Economic Development'. *Journal of Monetary Economics*, 50 (1), 3–39.

EBRD (2007). *Life in Transition: A Survey of People's Attitude and Experiences*. London: European Bank for Reconstruction and Development.

Edwards, S. (1998). 'Openness, Productivity and Growth: What Do We Really Know?'. *Economic Journal*, 108, 383–98.

Elvin, M. (1973). *The Pattern of the Chinese Past*. Stanford, CA: Stanford University Press.

Engels, F. (1877) [1962]. *Anti-Dühring*. Moscow: Foreign Languages Publishing House. Available from www.marxists.org/archive/marx/works/1877/anti-duhring/index.htm.

Engerman, S. L., and K. L. Sokoloff (1997). 'Factor Endowments, Institutions, and Differential Paths of Growth among New World Economies: A View from Economic Historians of the United States'. In S. Haber (ed.), *How Latin America Fell Behind*. Stanford, CA: Stanford University Press, 260–304.

—— (2005). 'The Evolution of Suffrage Institutions in the New World'. *Journal of Economic History*, 65 (4), 891–921.

Ericson, R. E. (1991). 'The Classical Soviet-type Economy: Nature of the System and Implications for Reform'. *Journal of Economic Perspectives*, 5 (4), 11–27.

Esfahani, H. S. (2000). 'Institutions and Government Controls'. *Journal of Development Economics*, 63 (2), 197–229.

Fei, J. C. H., G. Ranis and S. W. Y. Kuo, with the assistance of Y.-Y. Bian and J. Chang Collins (1979). *Growth with Equity: The Taiwan Case*. New York: Oxford University Press.

Frankel, J., and D. Romer (1999). 'Does Trade Cause Growth?' *American Economic Review*, 89 (3), 379–99.

Fraser Institute (2007). *Economic Freedom of the World 2007*. Vancouver: Fraser Institute.

Friedman, T. (2005). *The World Is Flat: A Brief History of the Twenty-first Century*. New York: Farrar, Straus and Giroux.

Fritz, V., and A. R. Menocal (2007). 'Developmental States in the New Millennium: Concepts and Challenges for a New Aid Agenda'. *Development Policy Review*, 25 (5), 531–52.

Frydman, R., C. W. Gary and A. Rapaczynski (eds.) (1996). *Corporate Governance in Central Europe and Russia*, vol. II, *Insiders and the State*. Budapest: Central European University Press.

Gerschenkron, A. (1962). *Economic Backwardness in Historical Perspective: A Book of Essays*. Cambridge, MA: Belknap Press of Harvard University Press.

Gordon, R., and W. Li (2005a). *Tax Structure in Developing Countries: Many Puzzles and a Possible Explanation*. Working Paper no. 11267. National Bureau of Economic Research, Cambridge, MA.

(2005b). 'Financial, Taxation, and Regulatory Structures in Developing Countries'. Mimeo. University of California, San Diego.

Gregory, P. R., and M. Harrison (2005). 'Allocation under Dictatorship: Research in Stalin's Archives'. *Journal of Economic Literature*, 43 (3), 721–61.

Gregory, P. R., and R. C. Stuart (2001). *Russian & Soviet Economic Structure and Performance* (7th edn.). Boston: Addison-Wesley.

Greif, A. (1994). 'Cultural Beliefs and the Organization of Society: Historical and Theoretical Reflections on Collectivist and Individualist Societies'. *Journal of Political Economy*, 102 (5), 912–50.

(2004). *Institutions: Theory and History*. Cambridge: Cambridge University Press.

Grossman, G. M., and E. Helpman (1994). 'Protection for Sale'. *American Economic Review*, 84 (4), 833–50.

(1996). 'Electoral Competition and Special Interest Politics'. *Review of Economic Studies*, 63 (2), 265–86.

(2001). *Special Interest Politics*. Cambridge, MA: MIT Press.

Grossman, S. J., and O. D. Hart (1986). 'The Costs and Benefits of Ownership: A Theory of Vertical and Lateral Integration'. *Journal of Political Economy*, 94 (4), 691–719.

Groves, T., Y. Hong, J. McMillan and B. Naughton (1994). 'Autonomy and Incentives in Chinese State Enterprises'. *Quarterly Journal of Economics*, 109 (1), 183–209.

Hall, R. E., and C. Jones (1999). 'Why Do Some Countries Produce So Much More Output per Worker than Others?'. *Quarterly Journal of Economics*, 114 (1), 83–116.

Hansen, G. D., and E. C. Prescott (2002). 'Malthus to Solow'. *American Economic Review*, 92 (4), 1205–17.

Hart, O. D., and J. Moore (1990). 'Property Rights and the Nature of the Firm'. *Journal of Political Economy*, 98 (6), 1119–58.

Hausmann, R., D. Rodrik and A. Velasco (2006). 'Getting the Diagnosis Right: A New Approach to Economic Reform'. *Finance and Development*, 43 (1), 12–15.

Hayami, Y., and Y. Godo (2005). *Development Economics: From the Poverty to the Wealth of Nations* (3rd edn.). Oxford: Oxford University Press.

Hayami, Y., and V. W. Ruttan (1985). *Agricultural Development: An International Perspective* (revised and expanded). Baltimore: Johns Hopkins University Press.

Heckscher, E. F., and B. Ohlin (1991). *Heckscher–Ohlin Trade Theory* (trans. ed., introd. H. Flam and M. J. Flanders). Cambridge, MA: MIT Press.

Hirschman, A. O. (1958). *The Strategy of Economic Development*. New Haven, CT: Yale University Press.

(1982). 'The Rise and Decline of Development Economics'. In M. Gersovitz and W. A. Lewis (eds.), *The Theory and Experience of Economic Development*. London: Allen and Unwin, 372–90.

Howitt, P., and R. P. McAfee (1988). 'Stability of Equilibria with Externalities'. *Quarterly Journal of Economics*, 103 (2), 261–77.

Ishmael, O. (2007). 'Socialist Ideology Takes New Roots in South America'. Venezuelanalysis.com, 29 January 2007, www.venezuelanalysis.com/analysis/2198.

Ito, T. (1998). 'Japanese Economic Development: Idiosyncratic or Universal?'. In J. Y. Lin (ed.), *Contemporary Economic Issues*, vol. I, *Regional Experience and System Reform*. London: Macmillan, 18–37.

Jefferson, G., and T. Rawski (1995). 'How Industrial Reform Worked in China: The Role of Innovation, Competition, and Property Rights'. *In Proceedings of the World Bank Annual Conference on Development Economics 1994*. Washington, DC: World Bank, 129–56.

Jefferson, G., T. Rawski and Y. Zheng (1992). 'Growth, Efficiency and Convergence in China's State and Collective Industry'. *Economic Development and Cultural Change*, 40 (2), 239–66.

Jones, B. F., and B. A. Olken (2005). 'Do Leaders Matter? National Leadership and Growth since World War II'. *Quarterly Journal of Economics*, 120 (3), 835–64.

Jones, E. L. (1981). *The European Miracle: Environments, Economies and Geopolitics in the History of Europe and Asia*. Cambridge: Cambridge University Press.

Kaufmann, D., A. Kraay and P. Zoido-Lobatón (2002). *Governance Matters II: Updated Indicators for 2000/01*, Policy Research Working Paper no. 2772. World Bank, Washington, DC.

Keynes, J. M. (1926). *The End of Laissez-faire*. London: Hogarth Press.

(1935) [1964]. *The General Theory of Employment, Interest, and Money*. New York: Harcourt, Brace and World.

Kim, Y. H. (1988). *Higashi Ajia Kogyoka to Sekai Shihonshugi* (*Industrialisation of East Asia and the World Capitalism*) (in Japanese). Tokyo: Toyo Keizai Shimpo-sha.

Kolodko, G. W. (2000). *From Shock to Therapy: The Political Economy of Postsocialist Transformation*. New York: Oxford University Press.

Kornai, J. (1986). 'The Soft Budget Constraint'. *Kyklos*, 39 (1), 3–30.

(1990). *The Road to a Free Economy*. New York: W. W. Norton.

(1992). *The Socialist System: The Political Economy of Communism*. Princeton, NJ: Princeton University Press.

Krueger, A. O. (1974). 'The Political Economy of Rent-seeking Society'. *American Economic Review*, 64 (3), 291–303.

(1990). 'Government Failures in Development'. *Journal of Economic Perspectives*, 4 (3), 9–23.

(1992). *Economic Policy Reforms in Developing Countries*. Oxford: Basil Blackwell.

(1995). 'Policy Lessons from Development Experience since the Second World War'. In J. R. Behrman and T. N. Srinivasan (eds.), *Handbook of Development Economics*, vol. III, part B. Amsterdam: Elsevier Science, 2497–550.

(1997). 'Trade Policy and Economic Development: How We Learn'. *American Economic Review*, 87 (1), 1–22.

Krugman, P. R. (1981). 'Trade, Accumulation and Uneven Development'. *Journal of Development Economics*, 8 (2), 149–61.

(1987). 'The Narrow Moving Band, the Dutch Disease, and the Competitive Consequences of Mrs Thatcher'. *Journal of Development Economics*, 27 (1/2), 41–55.

(1991). 'History versus Expectations'. *Quarterly Journal of Economics*, 106 (2), 651–67.

Krugman, P. R., and M. Obstfeld (1997). *International Economics: Theory and Policy* (4th edn.). New York: Addison-Wesley.

Kuczynsky, M., and R. L. Meek (1972). *Quesnay's Tableau Economique*. London: Macmillan.

Kuznets, S. (1966). *Modern Economic Growth: Rate, Structure and Spread*. New Haven, CT: Yale University Press.

Lal, D. (1983). *The Poverty of 'Development Economics'*. Cambridge, MA: Harvard University Press.

(1994). *Against Dirigisme: The Case for Unshackling Economic Markets*. San Francisco: ICS Press.

(1998). *Unintended Consequences: The Impact of Factor Endowments, Culture and Politics on Long-run Economic Performance*. Cambridge, MA: MIT Press.

(2005). *The Hindu Equilibrium: India c. 1500 B.C. – 2000 A.D.* (abridged and revised). Oxford: Oxford University Press.

Lal, D., and H. Myint (1996). *The Political Economy of Poverty, Equity and Growth: A Comparative Study*. Oxford: Clarendon Press.

Landes, D. S. (1969). *The Unbound Prometheus: Technological Change and Industrial Development in Western Europe from 1750 to the Present*. London: Cambridge University Press.

—— (1998). *The Wealth and Poverty of Nations: Why Some Are So Rich and Some So Poor*. New York: W. W. Norton.

Lau, L. J., Y. Qian and G. Roland (2000). 'Reform without Losers: An Interpretation of China's Dual-track Approach to Transition'. *Journal of Political Economy*, 108 (1), 120–43.

Lavigne, M. (1995). *The Economics of Transition: From Socialist Economy to Market Economy*. New York: St Martin's Press.

Lee, K. (2007). 'Making a Technological Catch-up: Barriers and Opportunities'. *Asian Journal of Technology Innovation*, 13 (2), 97–131.

Leibenstein, H. (1957). *Economic Backwardness and Economic Growth: Studies in the Theory of Economic Development*. New York: John Wiley.

Lenin, V. I. (1918) [1972]. 'The Immediate Tasks of the Soviet Government'. In R. Daglish (ed.), *Lenin Collected Works*, vol. XXVII, (trans. C. Dutt), (4th English edn.). Moscow: Progress, 235–77.

Lewis, A. (1955). *Theory of Economic Growth*. London: Allen and Unwin.

Li, D. D. (1996). 'A Theory of Ambiguous Property Rights in Transition Economies: The Case of the Chinese Non-state Sector'. *Journal of Comparative Economics*, 23 (1), 1–19.

Li, H. Y., L. Squire and H. Zou (1998). 'Explaining International and Intertemporal Variations in Income Inequality'. *Economic Journal*, 108, 26–43.

Li, W. (1997). 'The Impact of Economic Reform on the Performance of Chinese State Enterprises, 1980–89'. *Journal of Political Economy*, 105 (5), 1080–106.

Lin, J. Y. (1988). 'The Household Responsibility System in China's Agricultural Reform: A Theoretical and Empirical Study'. *Economic Development and Cultural Change*, 36 (3), Supplement, S199–S224.

—— (1989). 'An Economic Theory of Institutional Change: Induced and Imposed Change'. *Cato Journal*, 9 (1), 1–33.

—— (1990). 'Collectivization and China's Agricultural Crisis in 1959–1961'. *Journal of Political Economy*, 98 (6), 1228–52.

—— (1992). 'Rural Reforms and Agricultural Growth in China'. *American Economic Review*, 82 (1), 34–51.

—— (1995). 'The Needham Puzzle: Why the Industrial Revolution Did Not Originate in China'. *Economic Development and Cultural Change*, 41 (2), 269–92.

—— (2003). 'Development Strategy, Viability and Economic Convergence'. *Economic Development and Cultural Change*, 53 (2), 277–308.

Lin, J. Y., F. Cai and Z. Li (1994). *China's Miracle: Development Strategy and Economic Reform* (Chinese edn.). Shanghai: Shanghai Sanlian Press.

——(1996). 'The Lessons of China's Transition to a Market Economy'. *Cato Journal*, 16 (2), 201–31.

——(1998). 'Competition, Policy Burdens, and State-owned Enterprise Reform'. *American Economic Review, Papers and Proceedings of the Hundred and Tenth Annual Meeting of the American Economic Association*, 88 (2), 422–7.

——(2003). *China's Miracle: Development Strategy and Economic Reform* (rev. English edn.). Hong Kong: Chinese University of Hong Kong Press.

Lin, J. Y., and B. K. Chen (2007). 'Development Strategy, Financial Repression and Inequality'. Mimeo. China Center for Economic Research, Peking University.

Lin, J. Y., and Z. Y. Li (2008). 'Policy Burden, Privatization and Soft Budget Constraint'. *Journal of Comparative Economics*, 36 (1), 90–102.

Lin, J. Y., and M. X. Liu (2004). 'Development Strategy, Transition and Challenges of Development in Lagging Regions'. In F. Bourguignon and B. Pleskovic (eds.), *Annual World Bank Conference on Development Economics 2004: Accelerating Development (Bangalore Conference Proceedings)*. Washington, DC: World Bank, 197–223.

Lin, J. Y., M. X. Liu, S. Pan and P. Zhang (2007). 'Development Strategy, Viability, and Economic Institutions: The case of China'. In G. Mavroatas and A. Shorrocks (eds.), *Advancing Development: Core Themes in Global Economics*. New York: Palgrave Macmillan, 518–30.

Lin, J. Y., and P. L. Liu (2003). 'The Effect of Development Strategy on Equity and Efficiency' (in Chinese). *China Economic Quarterly*, 2 (2), 479–504.

——(2008). 'Achieving Equity and Efficiency Simultaneously in the Primary Distribution Stage in the People's Republic of China'. *Asian Development Review*, 25 (1–2), 34–57.

Lin, J. Y., and J. B. Nugent (1995). 'Institutions and Economic Development'. In J. R. Behrman and T. N. Srinivasan (eds.), *Handbook of Development Economics*, vol. III, part A. Amsterdam: Elsevier Science, 2301–70.

Lin, J. Y., and R. N. Ren (2007). 'East Asian Miracle Debate Revisited' (in Chinese). *Jingji Yanjiu (Economic Research Journal)*, 42 (8), 4–12.

Lin, J. Y., and G. Tan (1999). 'Policy Burdens, Accountability, and the Soft Budget Constraint'. *American Economic Review, Papers and Proceedings of the One Hundred Eleventh Annual Meeting of the American Economic Association*, 89 (2), 426–31.

Lin, J. Y., and D. T. Yang (2000). 'Food Availability, Entitlements and the Chinese Famine of 1959–61'. *Economic Journal*, 110, 136–58.

Lin, J. Y., and P. Zhang (2007). *Development Strategy, Optimal Industrial Structure and Economic Growth in Less Developed Countries*, CID Graduate Student and Postdoctoral Fellow Working Paper no. 19. Harvard University,

Cambridge, MA. Available from www.cid.harvard.edu/cidwp/grad/019. htm.

List, F. (1841) [1930]. *Das Nationale System der Politischen Ökonomie*, vol. VI, *Schriften, Reden, Briefe* (ed. A. Sommer). Berlin: Reinmar Hobbing.

Little, I. M. D. (1982). *Economic Development*. New York: Basic Books.

Lucas, R. E., Jr (1988). 'On the Mechanism of Economic Development'. *Journal of Monetary Economics*, 22, 3–42.

Maddison, A. (1995). *Monitoring the World Economy, 1820–1992*. Paris: Organisation for Economic Co-operation and Development.

(2006). *The World Economy*. Paris: Organisation for Economic Co-operation and Development.

Mao, Z. (1944) [1978]. 'Comrade Mao Tse-Tung Appeals for the Development of Industry to Defeat the Japanese Bandits'. In Joint Publications Research Service (ed. and trans.), *Collected Works of Mao Tse-Tung*, vol. IX. Arlington, VA: Joint Publications Research Service. Available from www.etext.org/Politics/MIM/classics/mao/cwcia/cwm9_1.pdf.

(1945) [1965]. 'On Coalition Government'. In *Selected Works of Mao Tse-Tung*, vol. III. Beijing: Foreign Languages Press, 205–70.

Marshall, A. (1920). *Principles of Economics* (8th edn.). London: Macmillan.

Marx, K. (1867–94) [1977–81]. *Capital: A Critique of Political Economy*, vols. I and II (introd. E. Mandel, trans. B. Fowkes), vol. III (trans. D. Fernbach). New York: Random House.

Marx, K., and F. Engels (1848) [1969]. 'The Communist Manifesto'. In *Marx/Engels Selected Works*, vol. I. Moscow: Progress, 98–137.

Matsuyama, K. (1991). 'Increasing Returns, Industrialization and Indeterminacy of Equilibrium'. *Quarterly Journal of Economics*, 106 (2), 616–50.

Maxcy, G. (1981). *The Multinational Motor Industry*. London: Croom Helm.

McKinnon, R. I. (1973). *Money and Capital in Economic Development*. Washington, DC: Brookings Institution.

(1993). *The Order of Economic Liberalization: Financial Control in the Transition to a Market Economy*. Baltimore: Johns Hopkins University Press.

(1995). 'Taxation, Money and Credit in the Transition from Central Planning'. In P. B. Rana and N. Hamid (eds.), *From Centrally Planned to Market Economies: The Asian Approach*, vol. I. Hong Kong: Oxford University Press, 35–72.

Mokyr, J. (1990). *The Lever of Riches: Technological Creativity and Economic Progress*. Oxford: Oxford University Press.

Moravcik, I. (1965). 'The Priority of Heavy Industry as an Objective of Soviet Economic Policy'. *Soviet Studies*, 17 (2), 245–51.

Morck, R., and B. Yeung (2004). 'Family Control and the Rent-seeking Society'. *Entrepreneurship: Theory and Practice*, 28 (4), 391–409.

Murphy, K. M., A. Shleifer and R. W. Vishny (1989). 'Industrialization and the Big Push'. *Journal of Political Economy*, 97 (5), 1003–26.

—— (1992). 'The Transition to a Market Economy: Pitfalls of Partial Reform'. *Quarterly Journal of Economics*, 107 (3), 889–906.

Myrdal, G. (1968). *Asian Drama: An Inquiry into the Poverty of Nations*. New York: Twentieth Century Fund.

Naughton, B. (1995). *Growing out of Plan: Chinese Economic Reform 1978–1993*. Cambridge: Cambridge University Press.

Needham, J. (1969). *The Grand Titration: Science and Society in East and West*. Toronto: University of Toronto Press.

Nehru, J. (1946). *The Discovery of India* (2nd edn.). Kolkata: Signet Press.

Nelson, R. (1956). 'A Theory of Low-level Equilibrium Trap in Underdeveloped Economics'. *American Economic Review*, 46 (5), 894–908.

Nolan, P. (1995). 'Political Economy and the Reform of Stalinism: The Chinese Puzzle'. In H. J. Chang and P. Nolan (eds.), *The Transformation of the Communist Economies*. London: Macmillan 400–17.

North, D. C. (1981). *Structure and Change in Economic History*. New York: W. W. Norton.

—— (1990). *Institutions, Institutional Change and Economic Performance*. Cambridge: Cambridge University Press.

—— (1994). 'Economic Performance through Time'. *American Economic Review*, 84 (3), 359–68.

—— (1996). 'Economic Performance through Time: The Limits to Knowledge'. EconWPA series Economic History. Available from http://ideas.repec.org/p/wpa/wuwpeh/9612004.html.

North, D. C., and R. P. Thomas (1973). *The Rise of the Western World: A New Economic History*. Cambridge: Cambridge University Press.

Nurkse, R. (1953). *Problems of Capital Formation in Underdeveloped Countries*. Oxford: Oxford University Press.

Ohlin, B. (1967). *Interregional and International Trade* (rev. edn.). Cambridge, MA: Harvard University Press.

Olson, M. (1982). *The Decline and Fall of Nations: Economic Growth, Stagflation and Social Rigidities*. New Haven, CT: Yale University Press.

Osborne, M. J., and A. Rubinstein (1994). *A Course in Game Theory*. Cambridge, MA: MIT Press.

Perkins, D. H. (1969). *Agricultural Development in China, 1368–1968*. Chicago: Aldine.

—— (1998). 'Reforming China's Economic System'. *Journal of Economic Literature*, 26 (2), 601–45.

Pigou, A. C. (1938). *The Economics of Welfare* (4th edn.). London: Macmillan.

Pleskovic, B. (1994). *Financial Policies in Socialist Countries in Transition*, Policy Research Working Paper no. 1242. World Bank, Washington, DC.

Political Risk Services (2007). *International Country Risk Guide*. East Syracuse, NY: Political Risk Services. Available from www.prsgroup.com.

Pomeranz, K. (2000). *The Great Divergence: China, Europe, and the Making of the Modern World Economy (Princeton Economic History of the Western World, vol. IV)*. Princeton, NJ: Princeton University Press.

Porter, M. E. (1990). *The Competitive Advantage of Nations*. New York: Free Press.

Prebisch, R. (1950). *The Economic Development of Latin America and Its Principal Problems*. New York: United Nations.

Putnam, R. D. (1993). *Making Democracy Work: Civic Traditions in Modern Italy*. Princeton, NJ: Princeton University Press.

Qian, Y. Y. (2003). 'How Reform Worked in China'. In D. Rodrik (ed.), *In Search of Prosperity: Analytic Narratives on Economic Growth*. Princeton, NJ: Princeton University Press, 297–333.

Rana, P., and N. Hamid (1995). *From Centrally Planned to Market Economies: The Asian Approach* (3 vols.). Oxford: Oxford University Press.

Ranis, G., and S. Mahmood (1992). *The Political Economy of Development Policy Change*. Oxford: Basil Blackwell.

Rawski, T. G. (1995). 'Implications of China's Reform Experience'. *China Quarterly*, 144, 1150–73.

Redding, S. (1999). 'Dynamic Comparative Advantage and the Welfare Effects of Trade'. *Oxford Economic Papers*, 51 (1), 15–39.

Rodríguez, F., and D. Rodrik (2001). 'Trade Policy and Economic Growth: A Skeptic's Guide to the Cross-national Literature'. In B. Bernanke and K. S. Rogoff (eds.), *NBER Macroeconomics Annual 2000*. Cambridge, MA: MIT Press, 261–324.

Rodrik, D. (1999). 'Where Did All the Growth Go? External Shocks, Social Conflict and Growth Collapses'. *Journal of Economic Growth*, 4 (4), 385–412.

(2003). 'Introduction: What Do We Learn from Country Narratives?'. In D. Rodrik (ed.), *In Search of Prosperity: Analytic Narratives on Economic Growth*. Princeton, NJ: Princeton University Press, 1–19.

(2005). 'Growth Strategies'. In P. Aghion and S. N. Durlauf (eds.), *Handbook of Economic Growth*, vol. I, part A. Amsterdam: Elsevier Science, 967–1014.

Roland, G. (2007). 'Understanding Institutional Change: Fast-moving and Slow-moving Institutions'. Mimeo. Department of Economics, University of California, Berkeley.

Romer, P. M. (1986). 'Increasing Returns and Long-run Growth'. *Journal of Political Economy*, 94 (5), 1002–37.

Rosenberg, N., and L. E. Birdzell (1986). *How the West Grew Rich: The Economic Transformation of the Industrial World*. New York: Basic Books.

Rosenstein-Rodan, P. N. (1943). 'Problems of Industralisation of Eastern and South-eastern Europe'. *Economic Journal*, 53 (3), 202–11.

Rostow, W. W. (1960). *The Stages of Economic Growth*. Cambridge: Cambridge University Press.

Sachs, J. D. (1992). 'Privatization in Russia: Some Lessons from Eastern Europe'. *American Economic Review*, 82 (2), 43–8.

—— (1993). *Poland's Jump to the Market Economy*. Cambridge, MA: MIT Press.

Sachs, J. D., and D. Lipton (1990). 'Poland's Economic Reform'. *Foreign Affairs*, 69 (3), 47–66.

Sachs, J. D., and A. M. Warner (1995). 'Economic Reform and the Process of Global Integration'. *Brookings Papers on Economic Activity*, 1, 1–118.

—— (1997). 'Fundamental Sources of Long-run Growth'. *American Economic Review, Papers and Proceedings of the Hundred and Fourth Annual Meeting of the American Economic Association*, 87 (2), 184–8.

—— (1999). 'The Big Push, Natural Resource Booms and Growth'. *Journal of Development Economics*, 59 (1), 43–76.

—— (2001). 'Natural Resources and Economic Development: The Curse of Natural Resources'. *European Economic Review*, 45 (4–6), 827–38.

Sachs, J. D., and W. T. Woo (1994). 'Structural Factors in the Economic Reforms of China, Eastern Europe and the Former Soviet Union'. *Economic Policy*, 18, 101–45.

Sachs, J. D., W. T. Woo and X. Yang (2000). 'Economic Reforms and Constitutional Transition'. *Annals of Economics and Finance*, 1 (2), 435–91.

Sah, R. K., and J. E. Stiglitz (1984). 'The Economics of Price Scissors'. *American Economic Review*, 74 (1), 125–38.

—— (1987a). 'Price Scissors and the Structure of the Economy'. *Quarterly Journal of Economics*, 102 (1), 109–34.

—— (1987b). 'The Taxation and Pricing of Agricultural and Industrial Goods in Developing Countries'. In D. Newbery and N. Stern (eds.), *The Theory of Taxation for Developing Countries*. New York: Oxford University Press, chap. 16.

Samuelson, P. A. (1978). 'International Trade and the Equalization of Factor Prices'. *Economic Journal*, 58, 163–84.

Schultz, T. W. (1964). *Transforming Traditional Agriculture*. New Haven, CT: Yale University Press.

—— (1977). 'Economics, Agriculture and the Political Economy'. In P. Anderou (ed.), *Agricultural and Economic Development of Poor Nations*. Nairobi: East African Literature Bureau, 254–65.

Shapley, L. S. (1953). 'A Value for n-Person Games'. In H. W. Kuhn and A. W. Tucker (eds.), *Contributions to the Theory of Games*, vol. II. Princeton, NJ: Princeton University Press, 307–17.

Shaw, E. S. (1973). *Financial Deepening in Economic Development*. New York: Oxford University Press.

Shinohara, M. (1982). *Industrial Growth, Trade and Dynamic Growth in the Japanese Economy*. Tokyo: Tokyo University Press.

Shiue, C. H., and W. Keller (2007). 'Markets in China and Europe on the Eve of the Industrial Revolution'. *American Economic Review*, 97 (4), 1189–216.

Shleifer, A., and R. W. Vishny (1992). 'Pervasive Shortages under Socialism'. *RAND Journal of Economics*, 23 (2), 237–46.

—— (1993). 'Corruption'. *Quarterly Journal of Economics*, 108 (3), 599–617.

—— (1994). 'Politicians and Firms'. *Quarterly Journal of Economics*, 109 (4), 995–1025.

—— (1998). *The Grabbing Hand: Government Pathologies and Their Cures*. Cambridge, MA: Harvard University Press.

Shubik, M. (1962). 'Incentives, Decentralized Control, the Assignment of Joint Costs and Internal Pricing'. *Management Science*, 8 (3), 325–43.

Singer, H. W. (1950). 'The Distribution of Gains between Borrowing and Investing Countries'. *American Economic Review*, 40, 473–85.

Smith, A. (1776) [1976]. *The Wealth of Nations*. Chicago: University of Chicago Press.

Sokoloff, K. L., and S. L. Engerman (2000). 'History Lessons: Institutions, Factor Endowments, and Paths of Development in the New World'. *Journal of Economic Perspectives*, 14 (3), 217–32.

Srinivasan, T. N. (1994). 'Development Economics, Then and Now'. In J. W. Gunning, H. Kox, W. Tims, and Y. de Wit (eds.), *Trade, Aid and Development: Essays in Honor of Hans Lindemann*. New York: St Martin's Press, 15–29.

Stark, D. (1996). 'Networks of Assets, Chains of Debt: Recombinant Property in Hungary'. In R. Frydman, C. W. Gary and A. Rapaczynski (eds.), *Corporate Governance in Central Europe and Russia*, vol. II, *Insiders and the State*. Budapest: Central European University Press, 108–50.

Stern, J. J., J. H. Kim, D. W. Perkins and J. H. Yoo (1995). *Industrialization and the State: The Korean Heavy and Chemical Drive*. Cambridge, MA: Harvard Institute for International Development and Korea Development Institute, distributed by Harvard University Press.

Stiglitz, J. E. (1989). 'On the Economic Role of the State'. In A. Heertje (ed.), *The Economic Role of the State*. Oxford: Basil Blackwell, 9–85.

—— (1994). *Whither Socialism?* Cambridge, MA: MIT Press.

—— (1998). *More Instruments and Broader Goals: Moving toward the Post-Washington Consensus*. Helsinki: United Nations University/World Institute for Development Economics Research.

Subramanian, A., and D. Roy (2003). 'Who Can Explain the Mauritian Miracle? Meade, Romer, Sachs, or Rodrik?'. In D. Rodrik (ed.), *In Search of Prosperity: Analytic Narratives on Economic Growth.* Princeton, NJ: Princeton University Press, 205–43.

Summers, L. (1994). 'Comment'. In O. J. Blanchard, K. A. Froot and J. Sachs (eds.), *The Transition in Eastern Europe,* vol. I. Chicago: University of Chicago Press, 252–3.

Sun, L. X. (1997). *Emergence of Unorthodox Ownership and Governance Structures in East Asia: An Alternative Transition Path,* Research for Action no. 38. World Institute of Development Economics Research, United Nations University, Helsinki.

Sun, Y.-S. (1929). *The International Development of China* (Shih yeh chi hua) (2nd edn.). New York: G. P. Putnam's Sons.

Teiwes, F. C., with W. Sun (1999). *China's Road to Disaster: Mao, Central Politicians, and Provincial Leaders in the Unfolding of the Great Leap Forward, 1955–1959.* Armonk, NY: M. E. Sharpe.

Teranishi, J. (1994). 'Japan's Way'. *Economic Policy,* 9 (19), Supplement, S137–S153.

Tsiang, S. C. (1984). 'Taiwan's Economic Miracle: Lessons in Economic Development'. In A. C. Harberger (ed.), *World Economic Growth: Case Studies of Developed and Developing Nations.* San Francisco: ICS Press, 301–25.

UNIDO (2002). *The International Yearbook of Industrial Statistics 2002.* Northampton, MA: Edward Elgar.

Veblen, T. (1915). *Imperial Germany and the Industrial Revolution.* New York: Macmillan.

Wade, R. (1990). *Governing the Market.* Princeton, NJ: Princeton University Press.

Weber, M. (1930). *The Protestant Ethic and the Spirit of Capitalism.* London: Allen and Unwin.

Weitzman, M. L., and C. G. Xu (1994). 'Chinese Township-village Enterprises as Vaguely Defined Cooperatives'. *Journal of Comparative Economics,* 18 (2), 121–45.

Wiles, P. (1995). 'Capitalism in the Eastern European Transition'. In H. J. Chang and P. Nolan (eds.), *The Transformation of the Communist Economies.* London: Macmillan, 46–77.

Williamson, J. (1989). 'What Washington Means by Policy Reform'. In J. Williamson (ed.), *Latin American Readjustment: How Much Has Happened?* Washington, DC: Institute for International Economics, 7–20.

Winter, E. (2002). 'The Shapley Value'. In R. J. Aumann and S. Hart (eds.), *Handbook of Game Theory,* vol. III. Amsterdam: Elsevier Science, 2025–54.

World Bank (1993). *The East Asian Miracle: Economic Growth and Public Policy.* Oxford: Oxford University Press.

(2002a). *Transition, the First Ten Years: Analysis and Lessons for Eastern Europe and the Former Soviet Union*. Washington, DC: World Bank.

(2002b). *World Development Indicators, 2002*. Washington, DC: World Bank.

Zhou, E. (1953) [1984]. 'Socialist Transformation and the State Capitalism'. In Department of United Fronts of Communist Party of China and Research Office for Documents of Communist Party of China (eds.), *Selected Works of Zhou Enlai on United Fronts*. Beijing: People's Press, 253–4.

Index